T5-BCF-417

3 2528 10109 5398

INCLUSION
POLICY AND PRACTICE

Thomas P. Lombardi
Editor

Phi Delta Kappa Educational Foundation
Bloomington, Indiana U.S.A

Cover design by
Victoria Voelker

Phi Delta Kappa Educational Foundation
408 North Union Street
Post Office Box 789
Bloomington, Indiana 47402-0789
U.S.A.

Printed in the United States of America

Library of Congress Catalog Card Number 99-67842
ISBN 0-87367-820-6
Copyright © 1999 by Thomas P. Lombardi
All rights reserved

This monograph is sponsored by those who have been touched by the leadership and service of a fellow Kappan, Past President A.G. "Woody" Clark.

Woody Clark embodied all that is admirable about Phi Delta Kappa International and served as a role model for those in the fraternity who continue to strive for excellence in leadership and service. He was first and foremost a professional educator who looked on his responsibilities of service to youth as his number-one priority. He promoted quality education in his various positions of teacher, coach, and administrator in the public schools and the Allegheny Intermediate Unit in Pennsylvania.

Woody's legacy to members of Phi Delta Kappa International is his unending quest for excellence in the association. He remained deeply committed to the importance of the chapters within the governance structure of Phi Delta Kappa International and the individual members in those chapters. His many contributions have left an indelible imprint on all who had the privilege of knowing and working with him. He certainly is missed, but never forgotten.

Past and Present District VI Area Coordinators

John Amato	Henri Belfon	Michael Dorgan
DeWayne Greenlee	Carol Mikulski	Frank Nappi Jr.
Roger Reynolds	Marilyn Richardson	Elizabeth Singer

Members of the 1998/2000 Board of Directors and Staff

Rayalene Brizendine	Sandra Crowther	James Fogarty
George Kersey	Richard Kolowski	Sherry Morgan
Eve Proffitt	Dennis Simmons	Ranny Singiser

Past Presidents and Special Friends

Douglas Bedient	Bessie Gabbard	Ronald Joekel
Gerald Leischuck	Carol O'Connell	John Rowley
	George Thomas	

TABLE OF CONTENTS

INTRODUCTION

Inclusion is controversial. Interest groups, politicians, and the general public have strong opinions on the practice. Many of those opinions are well-informed; some are not. Some want to change the way inclusion is conducted; some want to abolish the practice. Even educators disagree about how inclusion should be implemented and whether it should be done at all. Nonetheless, it is the law; and every educator at every level of schooling is affected. But it is more than just the law. It is the professional responsibility of every educator to provide each student with the best education possible. Inclusion, when done well, is an important means for meeting that responsibility.

Thus, in 1997, a dozen regional chapters of Phi Delta Kappa International conducted Leadership Skill Institutes for educators in the United States and Canada. The topic was "Inclusion: Its Impact and Ramifications on Education."

For many years, the Leadership Skill Institutes were supported by Phi Delta Kappa International and the Phi Delta Kappa Educational Foundation. These institutes were a biannual series of professional programs, usually conducted in the spring and fall, designed to help educators acquire the skills and strategies for dealing with specific professional issues that they were then facing and would likely continue to face for many years.

Although the institutes were supported by Phi Delta Kappa International and the Phi Delta Kappa Educational Foundation, they were planned and conducted by the local PDK chapters. It was the members of each chapter who found the resources needed to conduct their institutes. They conducted publicity, established budgets, and contracted for meeting halls, refreshments, and equipment. They joined with other organizations and sought out those who had something important to say about inclusion.

The result was that each institute represented a unique mix of viewpoints. Participants included researchers, parents, government officials, school administrators, teachers, college deans, graduate students, and teacher aides. These participants took a variety of perspectives: local, state, regional, national, and international. Their topics ranged from hands-on activities to philosophical visions. This book presents these various perspectives on the policies and practices that support an inclusion philosophy.

This book includes the presentations from three of those institutes, sponsored by the Columbia University, West Virginia University, and the University of Alberta Chapters.

In the first essay, Judith Huemann describes the trials, tribulations, and victories she experienced as one of the first teachers with a disability to be hired by the New York City public schools. Her early visions of what schooling for children with disabilities could be is beginning to be realized.

Stephen Levy and Joan Washington describe how collaboration between special and general education in two New York City schools has brought added benefits. When special educators have worked with general education teachers, they have brought strategies to the general classroom that have been especially effective for students at risk. As a result, there has been a significant rise in the scores on standardized tests.

Alan Gartner and Dorothy Kerzner Lipsky remind us that the intent of federal legislation was to create a unitary education system, instead of the dual system that had been in place for children with disabilities. The challenge of the Education of All Handicapped Children Act for free access to education has been met, but there are new challenges before us. Gartner and Lipsky emphasize that we must learn to see special education as a service, not as a placement.

Anne Smith, a research analyst with the U.S. Office of Special Education Programs, describes how the federal government is attempting to build the capacity for local schools to serve all students effectively. She notes that inclusion should make schools more pedagogically responsive to the diversity of their students, but that it is not easy to implement inclusive practices. Such implementation will involve systemic changes in the local, state, and federal education systems.

Fred West describes two tools that have been field tested and used in many classrooms in the United States and Canada. The first, the Levels of Intensity of Intervention Decision-Making Framework, helps educators to make effective decisions about instructional or curricular interventions. The second instrument, the Analysis of Classroom and Instructional Demands (ACID Test), identifies the important factors needed for any student, not just students with disabilities, to succeed in the classroom.

The next several essays describe inclusion programs in West Virginia. Senator Roman W. Prezioso Jr. describes the range of programs supported by the state legislature. Conrad Lundeen and DeEdra J. Lundeen report on the Collaborative Teaching program at Morgantown High School. And Holly A. Pae discusses how special education is woven into all core courses in West Virginia's five-year teacher training program.

Dorothea Fuqua, Patti Campbell, Kathy McCullough, and Pam Wilson offer seven steps designed to support functional skills instruction. They argue that a plan for acquiring functional skills should be part of every students Individualized Education Plan.

The final three essays were presented at the University of Alberta Chapter's institute. Dick Sobsey, Bev Ray, and Heather Raymond discuss inclusion in terms of vision, research, and strategies. They remind us not only that schools prepare students for the community, but that they also are essential parts of that community.

George Flynn offers a humanistic, almost spiritual view of inclusion. He argues that inclusion needs to be realized; it cannot be dictated, forced, or standardized. Thus inclusive classrooms are caring, joyful, active places where individual differences are celebrated.

In the final essay, I stress the importance of responsible inclusion. If community leaders, school administrators, teachers, parents, and students do not accept the responsibilities that come with inclusion, it will not be successful.

Editing this book proved to be harder than I thought it would be. I want to thank Donna Staggs, in particular, for her assistance in proofreading, scanning, and considerable retyping of the various essays.

Thomas P. Lombardi
West Virginia University

Inclusion: The Challenge, the Opportunity

by Judith E. Heumann

All teachers are — or soon will be — teaching in classrooms that include students with disabilities. Thus it is becoming increasingly unacceptable to limit the number of teachers in a school who have the skills to teach disabled students to only a few special education teachers. Regular education teachers, too, must know how to teach such students to read, write, communicate, and achieve to the highest educational standards.

As inclusion gains greater prominence in education, we will get beyond the necessity of referring to "inclusive" classrooms as if they were different from "ordinary" classrooms. In the near future, all classrooms should be inclusive, and we will no longer need the term.

Excellent education is education that is excellent for all. Children come from all racial, ethnic, and national origins and all economic backgrounds. And some children have disabilities. If our education system is to be excellent, it must be based on the premise that every student can learn, and it must encourage every student to have high expectations. If we are to prosper in the future, we cannot afford to waste the potential of *any* of our young people. America needs us all.

Judith E. Heumann is the Assistant Secretary, Office of Special Education and Rehabilitation Services, United States Department of Education. Heumann was among those who pioneered legislation that became the Individuals with Disabilities Education Act and helped draft and develop the Americans with Disabilities Act and Section 504 of the Rehabilitation Act. She also helped design legislation that led to the creation of 200 independent living centers nationwide. Her deep commitment to the goal of an inclusive society comes from her own experiences.

But the job is too big to be done by just one segment of the education community. Success demands that everyone in the education community work together to bring about the reforms needed to ensure that students with disabilities are given the excellent education they need and deserve. And the most important partners in these reforms are parents and teachers. Parents know their children's needs better than anyone else does, and educators know the methods and strategies for meeting those needs. When parents and teachers work together in effective partnerships, our children can be taught to achieve to the highest standards.

For more than four years, I have had the opportunity to visit schools across the country to see what works in educating children with disabilities. From this rewarding experience, I have developed my own personal predictor for success. It is leadership.

Where school leaders show commitment to educating all children and clearly communicate an expectation for high outcomes, that goal is being achieved. Where states send the clear message to school districts that programs should be based on the premise that all children can learn, children and youth with disabilities are rising to that challenge and are being included in ways that benefit them and their classmates.

Schools with principals who recognize the value of coupling special education's emphasis on individually designed instructional strategies with regular education's strong emphasis on challenging curricula have classrooms where all children are learning to higher academic standards. The results are demonstrable and impressive in those communities with school leaders who promote strong family/school connections and where leaders demonstrate an unswerving commitment to all families by making their schools accessible so that a small but important universe of disabled parents can fully participate.

For example, Mattingly Eisner, now a third-grader in Montgomery County, Maryland — near my home in Washington, D.C. — was born with Down Syndrome and multiple heart problems. Because of the IDEA, Matty has been able to obtain the education services he has needed during each phase of his young life.

From the time he was a newborn to the age of 18 months, Matty received early childhood development services at home because he had to undergo a series of open-heart operations and could not risk becoming infected by exposure to other people. From 18 months until age three, Matty went with his mother two days a week to a program that prepared him for preschool. Then he went to a preschool for children with special needs: three half-days a week to start and five full days a week later. Starting at age six, with kindergarten, Matty has been taught in regular classrooms with a teacher's aide to assist him.

From the time he began learning in an inclusive setting, Matty's ability to verbalize increased dramatically; and he has become an avid reader. Matty's teachers say he loves to learn and enjoys being challenged to learn new things.

Most of the children in Matty's school are from ethnic or racial minorities and have themselves felt "different" from the majority in our society. Nevertheless, some classmates used to tease Matty until teachers and Matty's mother helped the children appreciate his uniqueness. Now the children get impatient for their turn to study with him. Having Matty as a pal helps them learn important lessons about getting along with other people. According to his parents: "Because he's in an inclusive school, Matty has become your basic nine-year-old boy. He's loving and sweet, stubborn and playful. He's energetic, loves sports and music, makes up jokes, tells stories, and likes to play-act."

Before the passage of the IDEA, children like Matty Eisner were routinely isolated from the rest of society; their potential was ignored. But today, Matty is full of the anticipation and excitement that is the right of all nine-year-olds. He is formulating his life's dreams and expects to reach them. Matty serves as a model for the success of inclusion *with proper supports*. Matty — and millions of children like him — have benefited from the work we have been doing for decades.

I have a personal interest in such achievements. In the 1950s, I was one of the more than a million disabled children who were denied the right to go to school. I contracted polio when I was 18 months old. When I was five and ready for kindergarten, our neighborhood public school in Brooklyn would not take me because I used a wheelchair. Instead, the school system sent a tutor to my house twice a week. I received exactly 2½ hours of education a week!

Throughout my years as a student, the school system continually sent me and my parents the message that my prospects were limited and my future unimportant. But my mother and father were immigrants who truly believed that America was the land of opportunity. They always believed in their hearts that I had a right to an education that could help ensure a successful future.

However, there was no law to guarantee that right; so my parents soon learned that they had to fight for my right to achieve. When I was nine and in the fourth grade, I finally got to go to a real school. I was placed in a class hidden in a far corner of the basement. We were treated as second-class citizens. We were allowed to mix with the nondisabled children only on Fridays during schoolwide assemblies.

The message from the school was: Disabled children are not valued as people, and certainly not as students. The results were predictable: Very few of the children in my "special" class went on to further studies. In fact, I was the first student in my class to go to high school — but not until my parents fought for this right. If it were not for them, I would have gone back to home instruction after eighth grade.

I went on to college and became certified to teach in the New York City school system. But when I applied for a teaching license in that system, school officials turned down my application because I used a wheelchair. Again with the support of my parents, I decided to fight. Attorneys donated their services, and we sued the New York City school system using the guarantees against discrimination granted by the United States Constitution. My case came before the first black female to be appointed to a federal court, the great Constance Baker Motley. She ordered the New York City schools to give me a new medical test and, finally, I got my license. Then I had to fight for a job, because no one, it seemed, would hire me.

I finally got a teaching job in that same school basement where I had attended elementary school. I believe that I was the first disabled teacher those children had. I know that for many I was the only disabled professional person they had ever met. When I asked them what they wanted to be as adults, the only profession they named was teaching. This might have been a sign that they liked me as a teacher, but it also showed how limited their horizons were.

I still am very proud that my parents and hundreds of thousands of others waged a fight to open the schoolhouse doors for disabled children. I believe that this struggle will be viewed by history as reaffirming the fundamental right of all Americans to be free of discrimination and arbitrary treatment.

Today, the law says that every student in America must be given an equal opportunity for a quality education in the least restrictive setting possible. Every youngster who is disabled has a legal right to an education in an inclusive setting with appropriate supports. But the benefits of inclusion go far beyond legalities. An inclusive education benefits all children, those with disabilities and those who are not disabled.

All students in inclusive environments benefit from learning that human beings can vary greatly in appearance, background, and perspective and still have their humanity in common. By learning to study, play, and work with peers who have disabilities, nondisabled students gain lessons that will help them in later life, lessons of character that are just as valuable as the academic knowledge they gain.

If adequate supports and resources are provided, students with disabilities do better in inclusive settings because they are held to the highest possible standards of achievement. These students are more likely to get jobs, to earn higher salaries, and to participate fully in their communities.

It is important to keep in mind that inclusion also can offer a more efficient way to use resources to support the learning needs of a broader group of students, a very important factor in this era of shrinking budgets. Though limited research has been done in this area, some findings show equivalent or better achievement among nondisabled children who have had classmates with significant disabilities.

For example, I have been told about a disabled student who had very few communication skills who was placed in an inclusive class in Tulsa, Oklahoma. Before she got there, the children in the class had a reputation for being less than completely attentive in class. But when the disabled student arrived, the students took great pride in learning what she meant when she made various sounds and in interpreting her sounds to the teacher. In order to learn what their new classmate was saying, the students became quieter in class. By the end of the semester, everybody was learning more.

Inclusion must be meaningful if it is to succeed, and it must be done with proper and adequate supports and resources. Inclusion means more than just rearranging furniture or creating curb cuts. Inclusion requires a change in the culture of the school from the top down and the bottom up. It requires that principals and teachers assume responsibility for *all* students, that children with disabilities be viewed as full participants in their schools, and not as mere tokens. It also means that nondisabled students be taught, and then expected, to value the contributions that their disabled peers bring to the classroom experience.

For some students with significant disabilities, inclusion also can mean the provision of specialized services or education outside the regular class for a limited period of time. Indeed, across the country, there are discussions in virtually every school district about how to create programs that strike the correct balance between those needs that can be met only through separate education and those that can be met best through inclusive education. I believe that these debates are healthy and productive.

The move to inclusive educational practices is driven by a respect for diversity and a strong commitment to the rights of individuals with disabilities to be part of every community. One of the main goals of inclusive education must be to help disabled students maintain their sense of dignity and self-esteem. Most disabled students feel tremendous pressures to let go of their individuality and self-worth. In a thousand ways every day, society sends the message that because they are different, it is natural for them to be excluded.

But we can all help disabled students understand that this message is simply not true. Being disabled is just a way of being. It is not the way persons communicate, transport themselves from place to place, or sense the world that limits their ability to achieve — it is the way society reacts to these persons that limits them.

It is absolutely vital that students with disabilities have role models to whom they can relate; it is vital that students with disabilities see adults with disabilities engaged in a wide variety of professions and roles. It also is vital that students with disabilities have peer models with whom to identify.

Think for a moment about the books you used to learn how to read. Did they portray boys and girls with disabilities along with nondisabled children? Do teaching materials in general portray nondisabled people leading lives integrated with disabled people? Are students being taught about the contributions of such disabled people as President Franklin Roosevelt or Alexander Graham Bell or Stephen Hawking, who has uncovered the answers to some of the universe's deepest mysteries? Do students learn about Beethoven or Helen Keller? Do they even realize that these remarkable people were or are disabled? I hope so.

We must work with all students to overcome prejudice against disabled people. A recent Lou Harris poll showed that 74% of the people surveyed feel awkward, embarrassed, and generally uncomfortable in the company of people with disabilities; 47% feel fear.

This prejudice is just like any other: Children are not born with it; they learn it. But they do not have to learn it. For example, I visited a school in California that had been the focus of a major court battle over the question of whether or not to include a young disabled girl, Rachel, in a regular classroom. The case went from court to court, and eventually Rachel was allowed to sit with nondisabled children. When I visited the school after the case was

11

settled, one of Rachel's classmates asked me, "What's the big deal about Rachel being with us? Why couldn't she come here before?"

I think adults can learn a lot from that student's question. Just as she couldn't see the "big deal" about Rachel being in a regular class, most American students today — thank heavens — also cannot see the big deal about white and black children going to school together. In other words, inclusion is just another step toward bringing young people together so that they can lead lives free of prejudice.

Though our nation has made great progress over the last 20 or 30 years, disabled students still have a dropout rate over 35%. We must do better!

I would like to share five areas that the Clinton Administration believes must be addressed in order to improve educational results for children with disabilities.

First, High Expectations: We need to establish high expectations for disabled children, and we need to ensure that there is accountability for results. At the federal level, the Department of Education is pursuing this objective through implementation of the Government Performance and Results Act of 1993. We are in the process of identifying goals for each of our programs and developing performance indicators that will be used in gauging progress. In the area of special education, possible indicators would include the graduation rate, participation and performance on assessments, and such post-school results as employment and participation in community life.

At the state level, there should be a corresponding effort to develop goals and indicators for the performance of children with disabilities and to monitor progress toward achieving those goals. States should be analyzing their own data on graduation and dropout rates, performance on assessments, participation in post-secondary education, and positive employment outcomes. Of course, the purpose of all assessments should be to create tools for developing appropriate strategies for improvement.

Children with disabilities must be included in state and district assessments. Even though civil rights statutes prohibit arbitrary and discriminatory exclusion of students with disabilities from assessments, many states actually exclude half or more of these students. As a result, those excluded may be denied meaningful access to the curriculum to which these assessments are tied. One strategy for improving access to the general curriculum is to improve individualized education programs (IEPs). The IEP process also should be used as a means of ensuring that children with disabilities are provided the accommodations they need to participate in assessments. It is tragically obvious that states do not expect them to reach the same high standards as those established for nondisabled children.

Of course, a small percentage of children with significant cognitive disabilities cannot be appropriately included in regular assessments. In those rare cases, states and school districts should provide alternative assessments for these children. Furthermore, regular feedback to the parents of these children should be routine, just as it is for the parents of students who are not disabled.

Second, Services, Not Places: Each child's individual needs should be addressed in the least restrictive environment for that child. We must stop thinking about special education as a separate program and a separate place to put students; we must start thinking about special education in terms of the supports and services children need in whatever setting is the least restrictive, whether it is the regular classroom, a resource room, a separate classroom, or a separate school. A child should never be "dumped" in a setting in which the teacher is not equipped to address that child's special needs and in which the child is not provided with needed supports; yet all too often, we hear of that type of situation.

One strategy for achieving successful inclusion of children with disabilities in the regular classroom is to include a regular education teacher in the IEP meeting. This teacher would offer a perspective on what is possible in the regular class and what is needed for success. In addition, communication and collaboration between regular teachers and special education personnel is a key factor in successful inclusion. Moreover, appropriate training for both regular and special education teachers is essential to ensure that the needs of children with disabilities are met in the regular classroom.

Third, Due Process: Due process protections have been instrumental in ensuring equal educational opportunity for children with disabilities, and they must not be weakened. We wholeheartedly support the use of less adversarial mechanisms, such as mediation, to resolve disagreements between parents and schools. Unnecessary lawsuits create emotional and financial stress for parents and school districts. We believe that all parents should be offered the option of mediation in cases where a dispute exists. At the same time, the recognized right of parents to due process hearings to resolve disputes is central to implementation of the IDEA. The IDEA Amendments of 1997 require states, at a minimum, to offer mediation when a due process hearing is requested. However, its use is voluntary on the part of parents and school districts.

Fourth, Safe Schools: The Clinton Administration is committed to ensuring that our nation's schools are able to address discipline problems. Indeed, the IDEA Amendments of 1997 provide increased options for addressing disciplinary problems without undermining education service delivery to students with disabilities.

There still seems to be considerable misinformation about what disciplinary actions are permissible; these misperceptions need to be cleared up.

For the first time, the new law clarifies how school disciplinary rules fit with the obligation to provide a free appropriate public education to disabled children. The law explicitly requires that children who need it receive instruction and services to help them follow the rules and get along in school. However, the law also recognizes that if students bring a weapon or illegal drugs to school, schools have the right to remove children with disabilities to an alternative education setting for up to 45 days. The new law permits schools to go to a hearing officer for an injunction to remove children for up to 45 days if they are considered substantially likely to injure themselves or others. Previously, only a court had that authority. And the law also recognizes the right of schools to report crimes to law enforcement or judicial authorities. At the same time, the law guarantees that children under suspension or expulsion would still receive special education services elsewhere.

A focus on prevention also can make a big difference. There are many schools that have learned how to prevent violent and disruptive behavior through such means as identifying learning problems early, teaching peaceful resolution of conflicts, and developing behavior-management plans. We also know that student misconduct sometimes is caused when the child does not receive the necessary supports and services he or she needs in order to learn effectively. Children must not be penalized for the failures or shortcomings of our schools.

The law has been and remains very clear: Children with disabilities who have been suspended or expelled cannot be cut off from education services. This has been the federal government's consistent position since the Bush Administration. It is not necessary to cease the provision of education services to children in order to ensure safe and orderly classrooms that are conducive to learning, nor is cessation an effective form of punishment. We historically have opposed the cessation of services for children with disabilities because it reduces the odds that these children, who are among the least likely to return to school, will ever be productive, contributing members of their communities.

The following story illustrates the importance of adopting a positive approach in resolving these types of difficulties. Lincoln Elementary School, a Title I school, is located in downtown Salt Lake City, in Utah's most severely distressed neighborhood. Historically, the school had no innovative programs and no community or parent involvement. It was open only during the traditional hours of a school day. In four short years, Lincoln Elementary changed dramatically, thanks in large part to two programs built on IDEA-funded research and sponsored by the state of Utah. The programs were FACT, "Families and Agencies Coming Together," and BEST, "Behavioral and Educational Strategies for Teachers." Through these and other programs, the staff at Lincoln Elementary mobilized the surrounding community and formed collaborative partnerships with many professionals and parents. Lincoln now is open from early morning to late at night and has become a family resource center, as well as a school. Many creative and innovative programs now operate out of Lincoln, including the Kids Against Violence art program.

A child with a disability, whom I will call Eddy, is a Lincoln student with a history of physical and verbal aggression. He was known by both his classmates and teachers as the school bully. He was placed in the Kids Against Violence program, where he learned to be an expert potter; and he participated in numerous community service art projects. Today, Eddy's aggressive behaviors have almost disappeared. Instead of running from him, other children seek him out to help them on their art projects.

Fifth, Support Programs: A streamlined, comprehensive, and coordinated structure is needed for the effective administration of the IDEA support programs. The Individuals with Disabilities Education Act Amendments of 1997 contains six separate discretionary authorities, down from 14 in 1995, each of which addresses a specific identified need (State Improvement Grants, Research and Innovation, Technical Assistance and Dissemination, Personnel Preparation, Parent Information Centers, and Technology and Media Services).

We have refocused our discretionary efforts because we believe that the previous discretionary authorities were too fragmented and too narrowly focused; many activities were limited to particular age ranges or disabilities in ways that did not make sense. We believe that having fewer, better targeted authorities will simplify their administration and make results easier to measure. At the same time, we strongly believe that the underlying functions carried out by these discretionary authorities are central to the federal role in improving results for children with disabilities.

Meanwhile, we have good news to report: The 1997 appropriation for special education represents the largest annual funding increase since this program began more than 20 years ago. This increase, which amounts to $784 million (a 34% increase over the 1996 appropriation), presents a critical opportunity to improve education services for eligible children with disabilities throughout the country.

But the main point is that the community should work together in designing how to best use these funds. Our work together must be based on the fundamental concept that every student can learn. Almost every day a new study shows that all students can learn more than we thought they could. While different students require different teaching techniques, every student can learn. We must believe that no student is a throwaway child. Every student deserves a place in the least restrictive, most effective learning environment possible, with appropriate supports.

We also must recognize the need for additional training. When visiting recently with some teachers earning master's degrees in special education, I met a young teacher who told me she had asked her principal whether she could take into her class a kindergarten child that had been tossed out by three other teachers. Can you imagine that? A student had been rejected by three teachers, and he was just in kindergarten! The young teacher took the child into her classroom. Her teacher training had enabled her to work with this student and the others. All of this teacher's students are learning.

I know from firsthand experience that training is vital for all teachers, both in regular and special education. I have taught in a regular classroom in an inner-city school where one child rolled up like a ball in the corner and another was hyperactive. I had 36 children in that class. My first inclination was to think I should try to get these disruptive children out of my class, but I fought that feeling. I decided to learn how to teach my students so they could learn. I realized that if I did not teach these students, there might be no one else who would.

Inclusion: The Keyword Is Collaboration

by Stephen Levy and Joan Washington

New York City has two distinct education systems trying to exist side by side. The separation of general and special education systems means not only that services are duplicated but also that those services are delivered inefficiently and expensively. For one thing, too many layers of bureaucracy exist before services are actually delivered to the children. In addition, each system has separate constituencies with a multitude of special interests. Jobs, patronage, working conditions, power, and money make up the different agendas of those interested in maintaining the status quo.

Collaboration between these two systems is necessary, and that requires collegiality. Administrators must allocate planning time so that the participants can meet, plan, and work cooperatively. Administrators also have to put aside a block of time every week to meet with their counterparts, even if some of those meetings can take place only on the phone or by e-mail. The prime objective is to create a collaborative model.

At the Surfside School in Coney Island, Brooklyn, a collaborative model has grown and flourished for seven years. The

Stephen Levy is the general education principal of Surfside School and is a well-known speaker and practitioner of inclusive education. He has been honored by numerous organizations for his work in the field and has written several articles on the subject. His doctorate in special education is from Walden University.

Joan Washington is a school administrator and supervisor at Citywide Programs in New York City and has been supervisor of the District 75 Office of Inclusive Education. As assistant principal of Connie Lekas School, which is located in the same building as Surfside School, she was one of the initiators of the Surfside School's Inclusion Project. She has presented at numerous colleges, universities, and conferences throughout the country.

19

Surfside School is a general education school. The Connie Lekas School, a special education unit serving students with multiple and severe disabilities, is housed in the same building. Each school has its own principal.

In order to bring these two schools together, administrators arranged for the teachers to have collaborative planning time. They accomplished that by first dispersing one special education class among the general education classes at Surfside. That class comprised nine students, one teacher, and three paraprofessionals. The special education teacher, called the methods and resource (M&R) teacher, helped the general education teachers develop methods and strategies, provided in-class support, and provided indirect services by planning programs and consulting with general education staff and related service providers. Not having a classroom provided more flexibility by allowing this teacher to arrange for preparation periods at various times.

The collaboration between general and special education students has brought benefits to the entire school. Stephen Levy, principal of Surfside, credits a large part of the school's amazing rise on standardized reading and math tests to this collaboration. He states that the special education teachers have brought strategies to the mainstream that work beautifully with the at-risk population among general education students. Materials and resources, such as new math programs, computer software, and reading labs, are shared for the benefit of the entire student body. In addition, the extra personnel that inclusion brings to each classroom is a welcome addition for the often harried regular teachers.

An important part of collaboration is planning. The Surfside Inclusion Team meets monthly, or more often as needed, to discuss the students and their needs. The team consists of the general education principal, the general and special education assistant principals, teachers, prep teachers, parents, and related service providers. Participation at these meetings varies according to what is being discussed. Out of these meetings comes an understanding of how the system should function for the benefit of all the children and the changes and accommodations that have to be made.

Details that might otherwise be overlooked are addressed by the team. Because of inclusion, planning trips must take wheelchair accessibility into account; and even graduation rehearsal and prom sites must be chosen with an eye toward including all students.

Other schools in the area also have discovered that planning is the key to successful inclusion. For example, PS 77K is a school for students with autism and pervasive developmental disorders who range in age from four years old to 21 years old. The principal and assistant principal supervise full inclusion programs at four community school sites in Brooklyn and three sites where, it is hoped, integration activities will lead to full inclusion opportunities. The backbone of the inclusion initiatives at all of these sites is the commitment to planning time and collaboration on the part of the administration and teaching staff. This commitment is evident in the structured format of regular meetings held by three different groups: 1) the Student Planning Team, 2) the Administrative Team, and 3) the Inclusion/LRE Advisory Committee.

The Student Planning Team works through the daily issues and concerns that arise when students with disabilities are included in general education classes. The meetings are held at least weekly and cover all curriculum issues, adaptations, scheduling, support services, and such logistics as room arrangements, special furniture, and so on. The members generally include the general and special education teachers, a teacher assistant, and any other person who has an interest or expertise in the particular issue that is being addressed.

The Administrative Team involves both general and special education administrators. This team meets at least once a month to ensure that all the suggestions and requests made by the student planning team are explored and that they are implemented whenever they are found to be in the best interests of the children involved. Because the suggestions often involve changes in the system, the administrators must apply for exceptions from district policy and waivers from the state.

Finally, the Inclusion/LRE Advisory Committee meets every two months to bring all constituents involved in inclusion and integrative activities together to discuss ways to increase, refine, and enhance current initiatives. This committee includes all the teachers, paraprofessionals, administrators, related service providers, and a representative of each discipline. It is important to have parents and students also involved at this level. These meetings give everyone a chance to review the school's mission statement, set long- and short-term goals, and take a look at the bigger picture before determining next steps.

The results of this inclusion initiative have exceeded all expectations. The general education students are welcoming and supportive, and they are developing increased awareness and appreciation of differences among human beings. The students with disabilities have demonstrated tremendous growth in academic, communication, and social skills areas. PS 77K has expanded and modified the curriculum in order to close the gap between general and special education and continues to explore and develop inclusive opportunities at all levels.

Inclusive Education: Where Is It Going?

by Alan Gartner and Dorothy Kerzner Lipsky

In its summary, *Reauthorization of the Individuals with Disabilities Education Act* (1997), the New York State Education Department states:

> As a result of these amendments, the law now focuses on improving educational achievement and ensuring the success of students with disabilities in the general education curriculum. It emphasizes participation in statewide and district assessment programs and requires States to report the results to the U.S. Department of Education and the public. Finally, it severs the relationship between federal funding and the number of students identified [as having a disability].

In Section 601(c) of the Act, Congress finds that education of children with disabilities can be more effective when we:

- Have high expectations for such children.
- Ensure their access to the general education curriculum to the maximum extent possible.
- Strengthen the role of parents and families.

Alan Gartner is the dean for research at the Graduate School and University Center, City University of New York. Previously he served as executive director of the Division of Special Education, New York City Public Schools.

Dorothy Kerzner Lipsky is director of the National Center on Educational Restructuring and Inclusion (NCERI) at the Graduate School and University Center, University of New York. Previously she was superintendent of the Riverhead Long Island School District.

Gartner and Lipsky are the co-authors of three books and a score of articles concerning inclusive education and school restructuring.

- Coordinate IDEA with other school improvement efforts so that special education can become a service, rather than a place where children are sent.
- Support high-quality, intensive personnel development so that children are prepared to lead productive, independent adult lives.
- Provide incentives to whole-school approaches and prereferral intervention to reduce the need to label children in order to assess their learning needs.
- Focus on learning and teaching while reducing requirements that do not improve educational results.

In short, the education of students with disabilities is to be a part of a unitary — not dual — education system. Students with disabilities are to be full participants in the community and its education system.

This is a remarkable development. Without ever using the word "inclusion," the Congress and the President adopted legislation that has the potential to change education for students with disabilities equal to IDEA's predecessor, P.L. 94-142, "The Education for All Handicapped Children Act." Just as that 1975 law brought students with disabilities (then called handicaps) into the school house, the 1997 IDEA amendments provide the basis for making them full members of the school community. In the years to come, we are likely to hear less about LRE (least restrictive environment) and more about FAPE (free appropriate public education). In the future, school systems will need to focus on the goal of appropriateness — understood as providing the basis for achievement, consonant with that expected of students in general — in the context of full participation. Outcomes less than those for other children and services apart from them no longer will be accepted as the norm but, rather, will become matters to be explained and justified.

The 1997 IDEA amendments not only offer rhetorical connections between broad education reform efforts and needed changes in the education of students with disabilities, they also impose clear obligations on states and, through them, local school districts. These obligations include:

- States must establish performance goals, consistent with goals for all students in the state, and develop indicators to judge student progress. This was to be done by 1 January 1998.
- Students with disabilities are to be included in state and district assessments of student progress, with individual modifications and accommodations as needed. This also was to be done by 1 January 1998.
- For those students who cannot participate in such assessments, alternative assessments are to be developed and conducted. This is to be done by 2000.
- States are to report to the U.S. Department of Education and to the public on the assessment performance of students with disabilities, including those participating in alternative assessments. This was to begin on 1 January 1998.

These requirements necessitate major changes not simply in practice but in perspective, indeed, in values.

These requirements are a departure from the events of two decades ago. That is, in the deliberations prior to the passage of what became P.L. 94-142, there was contending testimony from professionals as to which students could "benefit" from education. Finally, Congress acted more on belief and ideology than on research — indeed, Congress seemed tired of the professionals' disputes and declared that *all* students are to be served, because *all* students can benefit. Now, in the 1997 IDEA amendments, Congress has declared that students with disabilities can learn, that the starting point is the body of knowledge "consistent" with that expected of all students, and that the outcomes of their learning are a matter of public concern and are to be incorporated in the overall results for a school, district, and state.

If students with disabilities are to be held to standards consistent with those for all students in the state, then the curriculum they are taught must be aligned with that for all students. And just as there may be modifications and accommodations in the measures of assessment, so, too, there may be differences in the instructional strategies, in providing what the law refers to as "supplemental aids and support services."

We are now at the opening of new era in the education of students with disabilities. They no longer are separate. That the words of the "full inclusionists," disdained only a few years ago as too radical, should now be adopted by the Congress, suggests how far and how quickly we have moved. Just as the teachers and administrators of the nation's schools made a reality of P.L. 94-142's requirement of access, they can, with the necessary support, make a reality of the 1997 amendments' requirement of quality achieved through inclusive practices.

Systemic Education Reform and School Inclusion

by Anne Smith

Change in education is influenced not only by new knowledge about teaching and learning but also by the social context of schooling. Within the United States, the context for current education reform includes such influences as increased cultural, ethnic, and linguistic diversity and economic competition in a global marketplace. And with the approach of the 21st century have come arguments about the mission and culture of our entire education system.

Since *A Nation at Risk* (National Commission on Excellence in Education) was published in 1983, many state and local leaders have undertaken school reform efforts. Most of the strategies to improve schools have had a "fix it" orientation — fix the parts, fix the people, fix the schools (Sashkin and Egermeier 1993).

Special education has been an exemplar of such fragmented efforts. Fuhrman (1994) notes that programs for students with special needs pull them away from both the mainstream curriculum and direct involvement with general education teachers and school administrators. Twenty-two years after the passage of the Education for All Handicapped Children Act (1975) — now the Individuals with Disabilities Education Act (1997) — attitudinal and architectural barriers continue to adversely influence how we educate students with disabilities. The law's least restrictive envi-

Anne Smith is a research analyst with the U.S. Office of Special Education Programs, Research to Practice Division. She serves as project officer and agency expert on the academic and social inclusion of students with severe disabilities. Before taking her current position, Smith was the state coordinator for the National Least Restrictive Environment (LRE) Network.

ronment (LRE) provision continues to be discussed, debated, and litigated.

That is changing. Once viewed by many as a *place*, special education is becoming an instructional support and an active partner in creating classrooms and schools to meet the diverse needs of today's students (Smith 1995).

Education should cultivate meaning. It should require both students and teachers to employ imagination, insight, and empathy. The segregation of special education students will not bring such excellence. Gilhool (1989) holds that the least restrictive environment provision of the law constitutes an "integration imperative."

The nature of school reform efforts is changing. Instead of the fragmented strategies of the past, the new orientation is toward systemic reform (Sashkin and Egermeier 1993). Systemic education reform departs from the specifically targeted efforts of the past in that it is designed to align policies and programs with expectations (Fuhrman 1994).

Historically, the mission of the U.S. Department of Education has been to ensure equal access to educational opportunity and to promote educational excellence throughout the nation. The inclusion of students with disabilities in general education classes with appropriate supports is consistent with this mission. Such inclusion also may make schools more pedagogically responsive to the natural diversity found in our school population.

Congress has recognized that segregating students with disabilities would not result in effective schooling. Thus it has passed legislation to encourage inclusion within a systemic reform of education.

Legislation and Discretionary Funding Programs

Goals 2000: Educate America Act. The Goals 2000 systemic education reform initiatives are intended to align curriculum standards and policy with expected outcomes and to develop accountability measures. The act targeted building the capacity to serve all students at the school and district levels and eliminating bureaucratic constraints to education improvement.

During the second year of Goals 2000 support (FY 95), funds were targeted for state and local implementation grants. These grants were intended to help states and communities increase student academic achievement, involve parents to a greater extent in schools, bring technology into the classroom, update teacher professional development, and create partnerships with businesses and community groups. Ninety percent of these funds went directly from the states to local school districts.

This initiative was structured to ensure that leadership from teachers, principals, and parents in schools informed the efforts of policy makers at local, state, and national levels. Neither top-down nor bottom-up reform alone is sufficient; both "ends" must collaborate to ensure that *all* students learn and meet higher expectations. Shared goals and a strong vision are central to the success of systemic reform.

Individuals with Disabilities Education Act Amendments. In June l997 President Clinton signed the Individuals with Disabilities Education Act (IDEA), which aimed to strengthen academic expectations and accountability for the nation's 5.4 million children with disabilities and to bridge the gap that too often exists between the regular curriculum and what these children learn.

The reauthorized IDEA is a substantial revision of this legislation. It is based on lessons learned about equity and excellence in education and reflects six principles that match the efforts of Goals 2000.

1. Connect the IDEA with state and local education improvement efforts so that students with disabilities can benefit from them.
2. Improve educational results for students with disabilities through higher expectations and meaningful access to the general curriculum, to the maximum extent appropriate.
3. Address individual needs in the least restrictive environment for the student.
4. Provide families and teachers, those closest to the students, with the knowledge and training to effectively support students' learning.

5. Focus on teaching and learning.
6. Strengthen early intervention to ensure that every child starts school ready to learn.

IDEA Discretionary Funding Programs. The Office of Special Education Programs (OSEP) recognized that "building the capacity of local schools to serve all students" could be conceptualized as either an issue of enforcement of the LRE provisions of the law or as an issue of implementing best practice. OSEP's approach has included both monitoring and discretionary program activities (Bellamy 1987).

Frequently framed as a civil rights issue, the inclusion of students with disabilities has been furthered by citizen advocacy, legislation, and litigation. Confronted with school districts opposed to inclusion, some parents have used IDEA's procedural safeguards through due process and litigation to secure inclusive services. Although the ensuing legal battles with school districts are often adversarial, lengthy, and expensive, these parents strongly adhere to the belief expressed by Third Circuit Federal Judge John F. Gerry in *Oberti* v. *Clementon* (1992) that "inclusion is a right, not a privilege for a select few."

Many educators are perplexed by the use of legislation and litigation to change special education systems. They believe that real and enduring change cannot occur with top-down, legislative, and compliance-oriented mechanisms. If students with disabilities are to be included in schools, there must be a bottom-up effort that changes values concerning curricula, pedagogy, and belief about disability.

In 1986 the Office of Special Education and Rehabilitation Services proposed the Regular Education Initiative (Will 1986), encouraging special and general education to form a partnership to serve students with special needs in regular classrooms.

Toward this end, discretionary grants authorized by IDEA's Program for Children with Severe Disabilities have supported efforts to promote "bottom up" change, as well as efforts to widely disseminate this information to the field. Since 1987 the Office of Special Education Programs (OSEP) has directed discretionary grants toward two goals:

1. Expanding the field's vision of what services and outcomes are possible by supporting projects that extend our knowledge base; and
2. Working to make this vision a reality by supporting activities fostering the development, adoption, and implementation of improved practices (Safer 1989).

These goals have guided the design of discretionary grant procurement strategies in three broad areas: knowledge development, capacity building, and collaboration.

Discretionary grant procurement strategies supporting school change and inclusion have included Statewide Systems Change projects, research and demonstration projects, and institutes.

The Statewide Systems Change projects were designed to encourage large-scale adoption of effective educational practices across state systems and to increase the movement of students with disabilities from segregated to integrated to inclusive school campuses. Statewide System Change projects have expanded both the knowledge and experiential base of student, parent, and professional networks committed to inclusion. These efforts also have produced increased momentum for change from segregated services in many state and local education agencies across the nation.

The priority to fund three-year research and demonstration projects to examine the academic and social inclusion of students with severe disabilities in general education classes was established in FY 89. Among the critical implementation issues projects had to address were:

1. Creating innovative staffing procedures to ensure adequate support in the regular education class and to develop an appropriate number and size of small-group learning opportunities.
2. Discovering how support staffing patterns in inclusive education settings change over time and across elementary grade levels.

3. Determining which types of small-group activities are associated with positive student learning outcomes.
4. Learning how to balance the instructional needs of students with severe disabilities across the instructional day.
5. Determining the conditions and supports required for successful full-time inclusion of children with disabilities in general education classrooms.

Finally, three 5-year institutes were supported with discretionary funds between 1987 and 1997. California Research Institute (CRI) of San Francisco State University received the first award in FY 87. Their activities became a major component of a federal strategy to translate research into state-of-the-art integration practices through development, validation, dissemination, and technical assistance activities (Smith 1992).

In FY 92 the Consortium for Collaborative Research on Social Relationships received the second five-year institute award to investigate social relationships through an interrelated series of descriptive and intervention research studies using quantitative and qualitative methods with an action research process design.

Lessons Learned

The discretionary projects taught us that the notion of "inclusion" is slippery. Its meaning depends on more than just a description of events or conditions; its meaning also depends on the beliefs of those involved in the experience (Smith 1995).

We have learned that strategies to promote inclusive school environments and bottom-up change are vitally connected to the context and culture of the school. Although top-down administrative support is essential, coercion is not an effective strategy for durable change and improvement.

We have learned that the concept of "school membership" is an important aspect of student inclusion in the school community. Having a student with disabilities move in and out of the general education classroom disrupts the class and contributes to the child being viewed as a "visitor," rather than as a "class member"

(Smith 1995). Thus for students to be included meaningfully, inclusion must be an integral component of systemic reform, rather than merely an "add on."

Preliminary findings of the Consortium for Collaborative Research on Social Relationships (CCR) provide evidence of reciprocal benefits for nondisabled children as a function of their social relationships with peers with severe disabilities, though these benefits may be highly individualized, that is, different for different people.

During a 3 March 1994 site review, CCR personnel noted that better understanding of these reciprocal benefits also helps us understand various motivations for promoting inclusion, for example, parents who want their child to have a friend or friends while the principal is more interested in promoting a social good.

We have learned that barriers to school improvement exist both inside and outside the education system. Within schools, there is tension as new practices and roles collide with traditional methods of instruction and professional turf. Other barriers, such as poverty, racism, political conflicts, and human resistance to change, go far beyond school walls (David and Goren 1993).

We have learned a great deal in the years since the passage of the Education for All Handicapped Children Act. The reauthorization of the Individuals with Disabilities Education Act has forced us to acknowledge that implementing inclusive school practices requires a systemic approach at the federal, state, and local levels. Rights, public policy, attitudes, values, pedagogy, and innovative strategies are interrelated and must be aligned (Smith 1997).

References

Bellamy, G.T. "The OSEP Plan for LRE: Schools Are for Everybody!" In *Proceedings of the National Leadership Conference 1987. Least Restrictive Environment: Commitment to Implementation*, edited by B. Wilcox and M. Irwin. Bloomington, Ind.: Institute for the Study of Developmental Disabilities, Indiana University, 1987.

David, J., and Goren, P. *Transforming Education: Overcoming Barriers*. Washington, D.C.; National Governors' Association, 1993.

Fuhrman, S. "Politics and Systemic Education Reform." *CPRE Policy Briefs*. New Brunswick, N.J.: Consortium for Policy Research in Education, Eagleton Institute of Politics, Rutgers University, 1994.

Gilhool, T. "The Right to an Effective Education: From Brown to P.L. 94-142 and Beyond." In *Beyond Separate Education: Quality Education for All*, edited by D.K. Lipsky and A. Gartner. Baltimore: Paul H. Brookes, 1989.

National Commission on Excellence in Education. *A Nation at Risk: The Imperative for Educational Reform*. Washington, D.C.: U.S. Government Printing Office, 1983.

Safer, N. "Achieving Important Outcomes." Presentation at the Severely Handicapped Branch Project Directors Meeting, U.S. Department of Education, Washington, D.C., November 1989.

Sashkin, M., and Egermeier, J. *School Change Models and Processes: A Review and Synthesis of Research and Practice*. Washington, D.C.: U.S. Department of Education, 1993.

Smith, A. "Five Years Later: A Project Officer's Perspective on the Research Institute on the Integration and Placement of Students with Severe Disabilities." *Strategies* 3, no. 4 (1992).

Smith, A. "From Miracle Workers to Teachers: Where We Have Been and Where We Are Going." In *Welcoming Students Who Are Deaf-Blind into Typical Classrooms*, edited by N. Haring and L. Romer. Baltimore: Paul H. Brookes, 1995.

Smith, A. "Systemic Education Reform and School Inclusion: A View from a Washington Office Window." *Education and Treatment of Children* 20, no. 1 (1997): 7-20.

Will, M. *Educating Students with Learning Problems: A Shared Responsibility*. Washington, D.C.: U.S. Department of Education, Office of Special Education and Rehabilitation Services, 1986.

Making Effective Instructional Decisions in Inclusive Settings

by Fred West

Frequently, the decisions that educators make regarding appropriate instructional, curricular, or behavioral interventions for students with special needs have been based primarily on the "places" (for example, Title I room, special education resource room) or "programs" (for example, remedial reading program, dropout prevention program) where the students are to be educated. However, students with special needs increasingly are being included in general classroom environments.

One difficulty with inclusion is that the interventions made to meet an individual student's special needs often have been more intrusive than is necessary. However, there are two practical tools to assist general and special educators, working collaboratively, to make effective instructional decisions for students with special needs in the general classroom. The first tool is a Levels of Intensity of Intervention Decision-Making Framework that may be used by individuals or teams to make effective decisions regarding instructional or curricular interventions for students with special learning challenges. The second tool is the Analysis of Classroom and Instructional Demands (ACID Test), which is an inventory that identifies the demands and expectations of a specific

Fred West is the director of Exceptional Student Education, Lee County School District, Fort Myers, Florida. He is the author of numerous articles and books, including Collaboration in the Schools, Effective Instruction of Difficult-to-Teach Students, *and* The ACID Test (Analysis of Classroom and Instructional Demands). *West is a frequent keynote speaker at international, national, and state conferences on the education of students with special needs.*

classroom environment. The ACID Test is used for intervention planning with an individual student who is receiving education services in that classroom.

Guidelines for Using the Framework

Intensity of intervention may be defined as the type, extent, and content of specialized instruction needed for the targeted student and the relative responsibilities of the classroom teacher, remedial or special education teacher, and other support staff or parents needed to implement the interventions. The Levels of Intensity of Intervention Decision-Making Framework requires users to specify the role of each person who will be responsible for implementing the interventions.

The following eight assumptions guide the use of the decision-making framework. First, as opposed to commonly used continua of services frameworks, this framework is not a static model that places students in specialized "places" or predefined instructional programs. Instead, this framework (see Figure 1) is a dynamic one that assumes that the instructional process will move students to more advanced levels of learning and, consequently, to less intense levels of intervention.

Second, the framework uses questions, rather than statements, to remind users that these intervention levels are not used as placements but as temporary instructional levels with the goal of moving the student with special needs as close as is appropriate to Level 1 (a general classroom program of instruction with no additional adaptations, modifications, or supports). Note that there is no mention anywhere in the decision-making framework as to where interventions are to be implemented.

Third, the levels are developmental in nature, with Level 1 being least intensive and Level 7 being the most intensive intervention levels.

Fourth, the questions in the framework assist in determining both the initial and ongoing extent and complexity of specialized intervention, as well as the relative responsibilities of those who will implement the intervention.

36

```
┌─────────────────────────────────────────────────────────────┐
│                         Figure 1.                           │
│      Levels of Intensity of Intervention Decision-Making Framework │
│                                                             │
│ Level 1.  What can be learned in the general program of instruction to the │
│           same performance standard as required of normally achieving stu- │
│           dents?                                            │
│                                                             │
│ Level 2.  What can be learned with normally achieving peers, but with adjust- │
│           ments in performance standards (for example, task mastery or │
│           grading criteria) according to the student's needs as determined │
│           through curriculum-based and portfolio assessment? │
│                                                             │
│ Level 3.  What can be learned with adaptations in instructional procedures, │
│           activities, materials, techniques, or tasks, provided with consultative │
│           support to the general classroom teacher?          │
│                                                             │
│ Level 4.  What can be learned with adaptations in instructional procedures, │
│           activities, materials, techniques, or tasks, provided jointly by gener- │
│           al classroom and support staff?                    │
│                                                             │
│ Level 5.  What can be learned with adaptations in the content of the general │
│           classroom curriculum to be taught jointly by general classroom and │
│           support staff?                                     │
│                                                             │
│ Level 6.  What curriculum or instruction must be adapted substantially and │
│           taught primarily by support staff?                 │
│                                                             │
│ Level 7.  What are those few situations in which the general classroom cur- │
│           riculum is inappropriate? What is the alternative curriculum or │
│           instructional program, taught primarily by support staff, that is │
│           appropriate for the instructional needs of the student? │
│                                                             │
│ From J.F. West, L. Idol, and G. Cannon, Collaboration in the Schools: │
│ Communicating, Interacting, and Problem Solving. Instructor's Manual │
│ (Austin, Texas: PRO-ED, 1989), p. 86. Reprinted by permission. │
└─────────────────────────────────────────────────────────────┘
```

Fifth, the questions in the framework should be addressed for each instructional and curricular area in which the student is experiencing difficulty. For example, Level 2 intervention may be appropriate for math, while Level 4 may be needed to meet the student's needs in reading.

Sixth, the process of matching the student's individual needs with the appropriate levels of intensity of intervention allows the student to progress efficiently to less intensive levels as skills are mastered.

Seventh, the framework is a tool to enable educators to use a collaborative/consultative process to make appropriate decisions regarding students' instructional needs in all education environments.

Eighth, the concept of performance discrepancy, based on the demands of the general classroom, is used as the standard for determining the appropriate level of intensity of interventions for each student in each area of curriculum or instruction.

The framework presents a continuum of intensity from indirect to direct support. Adaptations or modifications to curriculum and instruction range from simple adjustment of performance standards or mastery criteria by the general classroom teacher to those that are totally different in their goals, scope and sequence, and activities from the standards of the general classroom. Each decision should reflect the least intrusive use of support staff in meeting the student's learning needs.

For example, many students' needs can be met with indirect consultative support to the classroom teacher, rather than more intrusive, direct interventions, such as those required by cooperative teaching. Thus in the first three levels of the framework, primary responsibility for instruction remains with the classroom teacher. Shared instructional responsibility (though not necessarily a 50/50 split) by the classroom teacher and support staff is specified in Levels 4 and 5.

Levels 1 through 4 provide for various levels of adaptation or modification in performance standards, pacing, or method of instruction in the general classroom. It is not until Level 5 in the framework that the severity of the learning problem requires adaptation in the *content* of the curriculum or program; and even at Level 5, instruction continues to be provided at least partially in the general classroom and remains the joint responsibility of the classroom teacher and support staff.

At Levels 6 and 7 support staff typically are given primary instructional responsibility for meeting the student's educational needs. However, Level 6 does not preclude involvement of the classroom teacher. Level 7 depicts the few situations in which the general program of instruction is inappropriate for an individual student. In such cases, the team should specify the appropriate alternative curriculum or program (for example, life skills, inde-

38

pendent living, self-care) along with appropriate staff implementation responsibilities.

While the framework seems straightforward, we have found that even well-trained school teams do not always make consistent decisions regarding the appropriate levels of intervention for students, even when the student assessment data are identical. Possible factors that may affect these decisions include:

1. The discrepancy between the student's current performance in a basic skill or content area and the actual instructional demands or standards of the general classroom teacher.
2. The ability and willingness of the classroom teacher to adapt curriculum and instruction for an individual student or small group of students.
3. The extent to which support staff can design curricular or instructional adaptations that are feasible for effective implementation in the general classroom.
4. The number of students with significant learning difficulties in the general classroom.
5. The complexity and volume of "teacher-pleasing behaviors" required of a student by the teacher for a student to "make it" in a given classroom.
6. The types and scope of support services available to assist general classroom teachers in addressing the needs of difficult-to-teach students.
7. The existence of a structured, collaborative, decision-making and problem-solving process and well-trained staff to implement it.
8. Adequate opportunities for staff collaboration and consultation as a component of their professional roles.
9. Availability of appropriate materials, media, and equipment for students with special needs.
10. A school staff, building administrator, and parents that actively support the concept of educating students in the most enabling and productive instructional environment.

The ACID Test: Purposes, Content, and Format

Another tool that can be used by educators for effective instructional planning for students with special needs is the Analysis of Classroom and Instructional Demands (ACID Test). The ACID Test is a practical inventory that identifies a number of factors that are critical for a student to perform adequately in a specific classroom. Those factors include the teacher's expectations and instructional demands and the behaviors required of the student in the classroom (sometimes called "teacher-pleasing behaviors"). The ACID Test is designed for use with students in grades 2 through 12.

The ACID Test can be completed by teacher self-reports, student self-reports, the report of an observer, or any combination of the above. This inventory is not designed as a teacher appraisal or evaluation instrument and should not be used for that purpose.

The ACID Test has nine inventory sections: 1) general classroom/school behaviors, 2) classroom rules-related behaviors, 3) instructional content/presentation-related behaviors, 4) assignment/project-related behaviors, 5) group-work behaviors, 6) textbook and supplemental materials use behaviors, 7) study skill behaviors, 8) test-related behaviors, and 9) grade-related behaviors. A separate section on intervention planning is included to provide a format for identifying specific target skills or behaviors for intervention and for developing specific intervention strategies to address individual student needs in relation to the demands of the specific classroom. Finally, a separate Student Worksheet for ACID Test Performance Monitoring is provided to assist individual students in monitoring their progress in improving targeted skills or behaviors in their classroom over the course of the school year.

The items in the ACID Test inventories describe specific skills or behaviors that commonly are considered as expectations or demands in general classrooms. Each skill or behavior is rated twice on 4-point scales. The first rating is of the importance of a skill or behavior for adequate performance in the classroom. The second rating describes the student's current performance or behavior. After the ratings are completed, the educator identifies specific skills or behaviors in which there are significant discrepancies between classroom expectations and the student's current performance. When there are several significant discrepancies between expectation and current performance within one area of the ACID Test, interventions usually are developed to help the student achieve the skills or behaviors needed for adequate performance in that specific classroom.

It important to focus on only one or two interventions at a time. Otherwise the student can be overwhelmed. In addition, when multiple interventions are implemented simultaneously, it can become impossible to determine if a specific intervention is effective.

The ACID Test also has been useful in assisting educators, parents, and students in several other important areas. First, the ACID Test has been used to assist teachers in transitioning students from pull-out settings by identifying the demands of the regular classroom and providing instruction in the resource program to assist the student in successful re-integration. Teachers also have used the ACID Test to transition students successfully to the next level in school (for example, elementary to middle school and middle school to high school). Educators identify the critical skills or behaviors needed at the next level of schooling and then provide direct instruction to assist students in consistently demonstrating those skills or behaviors before moving to the next level of schooling. Finally, the ACID Test has proven to be an excellent tool for communication and coordination of expectations and demands among grade-level teams, among content-area teams, and between teachers and parents.

In summary, the Levels of Intensity of Intervention Decision-Making Framework and the ACID Test are two practical tools that have been field-tested and used successfully in hundreds of classrooms throughout the United States and Canada. These tools will help educators and parents to make appropriate instructional decisions for students with special needs. When used appropriately, they can increase the quality of instructional decision making in the classroom for all students.

The Levels of Intensity of Intervention Decision-Making Framework and the ACID Test allow us to make appropriate educational decisions without the unnecessary references to the traditional labels we have attached to students in the past. These tools also help educators to avoid the inappropriate designation of interventions as "places," rather than as various intensities of supports and supplementary aids to the student.

Resources

West, J.F.; Idol, L.; and Cannon, G. *Collaboration in the Schools: Communicating, Interacting, and Problem Solving.* Austin, Texas: PRO-ED, 1989.

Idol, L., and West, J.F. *Effective Instruction of Difficult-to-Teach Students: An Inservice and Preservice Professional Development Program for Classroom, Remedial, and Special Education Teachers.* Austin, Texas: PRO-ED, 1993.

The Integration of Exceptional Students in West Virginia

by Senator Roman W. Prezioso Jr.

I have seen remarkable changes in education in our state. West Virginia has embarked on a movement of total systemic change in both public and higher education. To give you a brief history of the education movement and tell you how our state hopes to prepare its students to meet the needs of a worldwide economy, I want to take you back to 1982, when West Virginia had its system of funding public education declared unconstitutional.

The Recht decision required the state to reconceptualize its system under the principles of excellence and equity and to rewrite policy standards by which the school system could operate. Can you imagine the ramifications of that decision and the chaos that followed?

West Virginia used this opportunity to develop a new beginning. A partnership was born between the business leaders, the state legislature, and the executive office, educators, and the citizens. They designed a series of initiatives that would build a foundation on which a new and invigorated school system could be established. For the past dozen or so years, the attention of these groups was focused on improving educational opportunities for youth and adults.

Senator Roman W. Prezioso Jr. is administrator of Adult and Community Education for the Marion County Board of Education, Fairmont, West Virginia. As a legislator, he chaired and served on many boards and committees, including the Elementary and Secondary Improvement Advisory, Education Commission of the States, House Education Committee (Chairman), and the Southern Regional Education Board. In 1992 he was selected as Legislator of the Year by the American Vocational Association and in 1996 was given Fairmont State College's Presidential Service Award and was elected to a four-year term as state senator.

In 1983 the West Virginia Education Fund, a nonprofit, private-sector group, was established to award small grants and provide monetary awards to teachers in recognition of outstanding performances. The fund began the process of forming partnerships between schools and businesses. Currently, 87% (780) of all the state's schools engage in these business partnerships.

To stimulate and support excellence of achievement by students and educators, the Governor's Honors Academy was established for gifted senior high school students and the Principals' Academy was begun to strengthen principals' abilities to serve as instructional leaders in their schools. In 1985 the Teachers' Academy was established to provide quality inservice programs for teachers. During that period, the major emphasis and the central focus was on equity and the curriculum.

By 1988 we had begun to move toward major systemic education reform. Teachers were empowered to have input into the daily function of their schools and faculty senates were mandated in each school by 1990. Teachers now had the vehicle to organize the areas of concern they deemed most important. School Improvement Councils also were developed to allow the community to have input and participation in their local schools. A major technology initiative was designed to position West Virginians to competitively enter into the next century and to compete in the worldwide economy. The technology initiatives in the public schools include:

Basic Skills Computers: This was a $70 million program that placed 12,000 work stations in grades K-4. We hope that by the turn of the century, West Virginia students will be the most computer-literate individuals in the nation. At this moment, West Virginia is the only state in the nation that has computer-literate kindergarten students.

The governor and the legislature did not just put hardware in our classrooms and expect teachers to teach with it — we understood the importance of training. Since the establishment of the Center for Professional Development, more than 10,500 teachers obtained inservice training to use this technology more effectively in their classrooms. The state of West Virginia entered into a partnership with Bell Atlantic called the World Schools Program. The objective of this venture is to connect all schools in West Virginia to the Internet Communications System.

West Virginia Education Information System (WVEIS): West Virginia began funding for this financial and management software initiative in the mid-1980s. The system provides administrative support and reduces the paperwork required by teachers.

Distance Learning and Bridging the Gap: More than 900 students in 300 schools were enrolled in distance learning courses last year. The Bridging the Gap Program uses the same technology to aid West Virginians desiring a college education who live too far from a campus to commute. Six rural school sites offer college courses after normal working hours.

Although education reform in West Virginia has been a positive experience for the most part, there have been growing pains. In order to bring teachers to the national average in pay, we have eliminated more than 2,500 teaching jobs. As difficult as that process was, it is widely accepted.

The most threatening concept to regular classroom teachers is "inclusion." School systems, including administrators, educators, parents, special interest groups, and legislators, have researched and debated the concepts of "least restrictive environment," "mainstreaming," "integrated education," and now "inclusion." All of these concepts have involved some form of participation by an exceptional student, both disabled and gifted, in a regular classroom.

The term "inclusion," which means "to contain," is not found in the state or federal code; and there is no universally accepted definition in the education community. Inclusion is a contemporary term that pertains to placing exceptional students in integrated classrooms. Even within the special education community, the interpretation of inclusion is not universal. There are two general areas of thought: The first involves a commitment to educate students with exceptionalities in the regular classroom. The second involves placing the student in a defined setting with the means to provide for the student's needs.

In the 1995 session the West Virginia Legislature addressed the issue of inclusion because of the unclear direction, the uncertainty of the mission, and the lack of guidelines in dealing with this highly sensitive issue. Only one thing was certain, the Education for All Handicapped Children Act of 1975, now called the Individuals with Disabilities Education Act of 1990 (IDEA), stipulates that children with disabilities must be provided a free public education in the least restrictive environment. The states must ensure that children with disabilities, including children in both public and private schools, are educated to the maximum extent with nondisabled children. Children can be placed in special classes or separate facilities only when the nature or severity of their disabilities is such that education in regular classes cannot be achieved satisfactorily with the use of supplementary aids and services.

Only after the stakeholders established these parameters and moved beyond this debate could legislation be passed to address the concerns of teachers, school administrators, and parents or guardians of the special needs student. The legislation mandated that each faculty senate develop a strategic plan to manage the integration of special needs students into the regular classroom at their respective schools. The strategic plan was then to be submitted to the superintendent of the county board of education by 30 June 1995 and periodically thereafter pursuant to guidelines developed by the state department of education. Each faculty senate was directed to encourage the participation of local school improvement councils, parents, and the community at large in the development of the strategic plan for each school.

Each strategic plan developed by the faculty senate had to include at least the following:

- A mission statement.
- Goals.
- Needs.

- Objectives and activities to implement plans relating to each goal.
- Work in progress to implement the strategic plan.
- Guidelines for the placement of additional staff into integrated classrooms to meet the needs of exceptional students without diminishing the services rendered to other students in integrated classrooms.
- Guidelines for implementation of collaborative planning and instruction.
- Training for all regular classroom teachers who serve students with exceptional needs in integrated classrooms.

Legislation requires that the regular classroom teacher be given needed support when a student with exceptional needs is placed into an integrated classroom. If the student's individualized education program requires an adjustment in either the curriculum, the instruction, or the service offered by the regular classroom teacher, the following support services must be provided:

Training for the classroom teacher must be provided pursuant to the integrated classroom program. In order to prepare the teacher to meet the exceptional needs of individual students, additional individualized training, pursuant to the rules developed by the state board of education, also will be provided if requested by the regular classroom teacher. Whenever possible, training should be provided prior to placement. When prior training is not possible, such training must be commenced no later than 10 days following placement of the student in the regular classroom. If there are unavoidable delays in providing training, the delay will not result in the exclusion of a special needs student from any class in the event the training cannot be provided within 10 days.

The regular classroom teacher must be given a signed copy of the individualized education program prior to or at the time of placing the special education student into the regular classroom. All of the student's teachers must participate in the development of that student's individualized education program and must also sign the individualized education program as developed. Any teacher disagreeing with the individualized education program committee's recommendation must file a written explanation outlining his or her disagreement or recommendation.

Referring teachers must participate in all eligibility committees and both referring and receiving teachers must participate in all individualized education program committees that might recommend possible placement of an exceptional student in an integrated classroom. The classroom teacher has the opportunity to reconvene the committee responsible for developing the individualized education program of the student with special needs. The meeting must include all persons involved in a student's individualized education program and must be held within 21 days of the time the request is made.

The classroom teacher is entitled to assistance from persons trained or certified to deal with a student's exceptional needs whenever such assistance is part of the student's individualized education program.

The legislation required each county board of education to use plans developed by the faculty senate to draw up a county strategic plan and to manage the integration of special needs students into the regular classroom. The county strategic plan was submitted to the state superintendent of schools before 1 October 1995.

Counties must file forms supplied by the office of the State Superintendent of Schools if they are receiving or requesting reimbursement from state-appropriated funds for the following:

- To maintain special schools, classes, or regular class programs.
- To have integrated classroom strategic plans and training related to integrated education.
- To have basic and specialized health care procedures, including the administration of medications, home-teaching, or visiting services.

All applications, annual reports, and such other reports as required by the state superintendent also must be on these forms.

As inclusion practices develop and evolve, continual program evaluation, additional teacher inservice, innovative curricula, and specialized support services need to be provided to assist all involved in the education of the special needs student.

Effectiveness of Mainstreaming with Collaborative Teaching: Third-Year Follow-Up

by Conrad Lundeen and DeEdra J. Lundeen

Traditionally, a resource/tutorial model has been used to deliver special education services to high school students in Monongalia County. Although these resource services may have been beneficial in improving their basic academic skills, performance of mainstreamed special education students in regular classes has remained poor.

In response to this failure Morgantown High School developed and implemented a "collaborative teaching" service delivery model during the 1992-93 school year. In this model special education students who enrolled in a specific subject were mainstreamed in a regular class with a regular teacher and regular students. A special educator was assigned to this classroom to team-teach the curriculum. The special and regular educators were jointly responsible for choosing teaching methods, curriculum formats, learning strategies, study skills, and evaluation methods for all students. The regular educator contributed his or her expertise in content matters; and the special educator contributed his or her expertise in learning, modification, and evaluation strategies.

Conrad Lundeen is an associate professor of audiology and chair of the Department of Speech Pathology and Audiology at West Virginia University. He has authored numerous demographic studies of school children with speech and hearing disorders.

DeEdra J. Lundeen is a special educator with certification in hearing impairment and learning disabilities. She developed and implemented an inclusion program at one of the largest high schools in West Virginia and has been teaching collaboratively with general teachers for seven years. Currently she is the director of special education for the Monongalia County Schools.

An analysis of student performance during the inaugural year of the Collaborative Teaching Program revealed that *all* students in the Collaborative Teaching Program performed equivalently, despite the substantially poorer reading comprehension scores of special education students. Furthermore, all students' grades improved after their enrollment in collaboratively taught classes. However, much of this grade improvement dissipated through the second half of the school year.

In order to determine whether the Collaborative Teaching Program remains an effective method for equalizing the academic successes of regular and special education students, we analyzed students' grades from the third year after the program's implementation. In that year, 11 different teaching teams used the Collaborative Teaching Program in social studies, English, math, science, and health classes.

Sixteen classes, covering five subject areas, were included in the Collaborative Teaching Program during the 1994-95 school year. Ten regular educators teamed with five special educators to teach 320 students (61% regular, 39% special). By far, the largest number of special education students were identified as learning disabled. However, the program included children with hearing impairment, behavior disorders, and mild mental impairment; a number of non-English-speaking students also were included in the program.

For each of four, nine-week grading periods an analysis of variance was performed on students' grades in the 16 experimental classrooms. Children with identified learning problems were assigned to one category, while those with no identified problems were assigned to another. Each class was treated as a separate level in the analysis so that factors unique to a specific classroom could be identified.

When the grades of special education students were compared with those earned by students with no identified learning problems, there was no significant difference between the grades reported for the two groups of students in the second, third, and fourth grading periods. However, the data for the first grading period do not conform to this pattern and require further analysis.

The Collaborative Teaching Program had mixed results in 1994-95. The preponderance of data showed that special education students and students with no identified learning problems earned essentially equivalent grades. However, the student grades in 1994-95 were substantially below those attained by students when the Collaborative Teaching Program was inaugurated in 1992-93.

Why were students' grades in the Collaborative Teaching Program generally poorer in 1994-95 than in 1992-93? It is certainly possible that the program's effectiveness had waned over the three years of its existence. However, there are other factors that might have contributed to a decline in scholastic performance.

For example, in 1994-95 the overall mean grades in the Collaborative Teaching Program were higher in English and lower in math classes. Five English and two math classes were collaboratively taught in 1994-95. The 1992-93 program, however, included six English classes and no math classes. This change in the type of course offerings probably contributed to the poorer grades recorded in the 1994-95 Collaborative Teaching Program.

Another possible contributor to the decline in students' grades is that Morgantown High School implemented block scheduling in 1994-95. Under block scheduling, courses met for 90-minute periods on alternate days, while classes met for 50-minute periods every day in 1992-93. The longer time spent in classes and the longer time between classes may have exacerbated the attention and retention problems common among students in the Collaborative Teaching Program, and thus may have affected their grades.

Despite these concerns, the Morgantown High School Collaborative Teaching Program remains an effective method for equalizing the scholastic achievement of regular and special education students.

West Virginia University's Teacher Training Inclusion Efforts

by Holly A. Pae

Special education's delivery of programs has changed. Schools no longer equate the instruction of students with disabilities with separate, "pull-out" programs; instead, most students with disabilities are now being taught in regular classrooms alongside their peers without disabilities. According to the *Seventh Annual Report to Congress* (U.S. Department of Education 1995), the percentage of students with disabilities aged 6-21 receiving services in regular classrooms in 1992-93 was 39.81%, as compared to 28.88% during the 1987-88 school year — an increase of nearly 11% in just five years. The percentage of students educated outside the regular school building dropped from 6.4% to 4.5% during the same period. This influx has had a tremendous impact on the role, expectations, and responsibilities of both general and special educators.

In addition, we also expect educators to be better able to meet the needs of an increasingly diverse cultural group of students. Concerns about how to educate students who are culturally divergent transcend many special education concerns (Madden et al. 1993). Teachers no longer can view their curriculum as an isolated, standard set of knowledge. Instead, they must tailor learning objectives to reach the variety of background experiences, learn-

Holly A. Pae earned her doctorate in special education from West Virginia University. She serves as practicum coordinator of teaching field experiences in the areas of learning disabilities, mental retardation, behavior disorders, and gifted education. A former special education teacher, Pae maintains an active research agenda. Her most recent publications appeared in Special Education Leadership Review *and* The Journal of Special Education.

ing styles, and interests of their students (Stainback and Stainback 1996). This shifts the focus of teaching to a child-centered model where all educators must identify and facilitate methods for actively engaging all students in their own learning. As such, teachers must create a classroom atmosphere in which all students can achieve their potential.

Unfortunately, with a few notable exceptions (for example, Feden and Clabaugh 1986; Kemple et al. 1994; Pasch et al. 1991), studies report that teacher training programs are not effectively preparing educators for their future classrooms. Given the increasing complexity of the student population, as well as the unprecedented fact that the culture of most novice teachers will differ from those of their students in the years to come, educators and education organizations repeatedly have called on higher education to restructure itself to better address these training needs.

The efficacy of the preparation of educators for teaching students with special needs in general education classes is particularly problematic (Fuchs and Fuchs 1995). Following the passage of the Education for All Handicapped Children Act, now renamed the Individuals with Disabilities Education Act, Congress funded a series of Dean's Grants across the country designed to better prepare general educators to meet the special needs of students with disabilities in regular classes. Despite these efforts, very few of the changes reported in the literature are well documented (Lombardi et al. 1982; Korinek and Laycock 1988). Furthermore, as Pugach (1996) observes, these projects were unsuccessful because they perpetuated the notion of a dual education system by creating isolated, separate general and special teacher training experiences. Establishing a separate training unit caused the program to lack coherence with or connection to the general scheme of teacher preparation's focus.

As a response to these concerns, West Virginia University, with support from a major Benedum Grant, has undertaken a sustained effort to restructure and redesign their teacher training program. Beginning in the summer of 1992, more than 250 faculty members and administrators from five schools and colleges at West

Virginia University and public schools in four county school systems established a forum to support collaborative interactions toward this endeavor. Over three years, this group identified and designed a five-year training model composed of three integrated parts: a liberal arts component, a teaching discipline component, and a pedagogy component. Guided by the program's set of research-based goals, students progress as cohort groups through a sequence of learning experiences. On successfully completing the program, students earn a bachelor's degree in a teaching discipline (for example, mathematics, English, history, etc.) and a master's degree in education.

The program integrates a special education strand throughout the student's training experience. The premise for developing this strand was the belief that if responsible inclusion is to be an integrated part of general education, then responsible inclusion also must be an integrated part of all teacher training. To accomplish this the program established a committee of special educators. The committee developed a list of learning outcomes related to responsible inclusion and expected of all future teachers graduating from West Virginia University. After agreeing on the outcome list, each of the members then analyzed the instructional content of the new program. They determined which outcomes were already in place in the existing core courses and assigned the remaining competencies to the most appropriate core courses. Finally, through consensus, the committee decided whether each competency was to be presented at an introductory level, a major coverage level, or an application level. In the end a new program emerged that embedded an integrated special education strand within and across each course.

This strand approach is quite different from other teacher training programs, which either require general educators to take a special education course in their training programs or incorporate special education modules in a few of their foundation classes (Swartz et al. 1991-92). Further, the focus of training is on specific teaching and learning situations, rather than on a broad philosophical discussion about inclusion. The university designed this program to address what teachers really want to know: how to meet the needs of specific students included in their classrooms (Roach 1995). It accomplishes this by integrating the special education strand throughout the entire teacher training experience to create a holistic, comprehensive approach to meeting the needs that teachers will have in their classrooms.

Another significant strength of the strand approach is that it includes a variety of student teaching experiences. As the students develop teaching skills and knowledge through their coursework at the university, they simultaneously participate in five different student teaching experiences at nearby schools. Through these experiences the students have the opportunity to demonstrate and apply under 'real life' conditions what they are learning. Because this process begins early in their training, it immediately engages the students to construct meaningful understandings about their learning and strengthens their abilities to accomplish assignments requiring greater complexity.

In addition, the program specifically requires the students to demonstrate competencies that are relevant to the instruction of pupils with special needs. For example, students must validate their abilities to collect, document, and analyze a pupil's performance for the identification of instructional goals and objectives appropriate for that individual. Other competencies include but are not limited to students demonstrating that they can adapt instructional materials, modify teaching techniques, and implement learning strategies. In at least one of their teaching placements students will attend School Based Assistance Team and Individual Education Plan meetings to further enhance their knowledge of special education practices.

It is hoped that West Virginia University's teacher training program will fully prepare our students to meet the challenges they will face as master teachers in the classrooms of the 21st century.

References

Feden, P.D., and Clabaugh, G.K. "The 'New Breed' Educator: A Rationale and Program for Combining Elementary and Special Education Teacher Preparation." *Teacher Education and Special Education* 9, no. 4 (1986): 180-89.

Fuchs, D., and Fuchs, L. "What's Special About Special Education?" *Phi Delta Kappan* 76, no. 7 (1995): 522-30.

Kemple, K.M.; Hartle, L.C.; Correa, V.I.; and Fox, L. "Preparing Teachers for Inclusive Education: The Development of a Unified Teacher Education Program in Early Childhood and Early Childhood Special Education." *Teacher Education and Special Education* 17, no. 1 (1994): 38-51.

Korinek, L.A., and Laycock, V.K. "Evidence in the Regular Education Initiative in Federally Funded Personnel Preparation Programs." *Teacher Education and Special Education* 11, no. 3 (1988): 95-102.

Lombardi, T.P.; Meadowcroft, P.; and Strasburger, R.J. "Modifying Teachers' Attitudes Towards and Knowledge of Mainstreaming Handicapped Students." *Exceptional Children* 48, no. 6 (1982): 544-45.

Madden, N.A.; Slavin, R.E.; Karweit, N.L.; Dolan, L.J.; and Wasil, B.A. "Success for All: Longitudinal Effects of a Restructuring Program for Inner-City Elementary Schools." *American Educational Research Journal* 30, no. 1 (1993): 123-48.

Pasch, S.H.; Pugach, M.C.; and Fox, R.G. "A Collaborative Structure for Institutional Change in Teacher Education." In *Changing the Practice of Teacher Education: The Role of the Knowledge Base*, edited by M.C. Pugach, H. Barnes, and L. Beckum. Washington, D.C.: American Association of Colleges for Teacher Education, 1991.

Pugach, M.C. "Unifying the Preparation of Prospective Teachers." In *Controversial Issues Confronting Special Education: Divergent Perspectives*, edited by W. Stainback and S. Stainback. Boston: Allyn & Bacon, 1996.

Roach, V. "Supporting Inclusion: Beyond the Rhetoric." *Phi Delta Kappan* 77, no. 4 (1995): 295-99.

Stainback, S., and Stainback, W. "Curriculum in Inclusive Classrooms." In *Inclusion: A Guide for Educators*, edited by S. Stainback and W. Stainback. Baltimore: Paul H. Brookes, 1996.

Swartz, S.L.; Hidalgo, J.F.; and Hays, P.A. "Teacher Preparation and the Regular Initiative." *Action in Teacher Education* 13 (Winter 1991-92): 55-61.

U.S. Department of Education. *To Assure the Free Appropriate Education of All Children with Disabilities: Seventh Annual Report to Congress on the Implementation of the Individuals with Disabilities Education Act.* Washington, D.C.: U.S. Government Printing Office, 1995.

A Road Map to Inclusion: Meeting Functional Curriculum Needs in Integrated Settings

by Dorothea Fuqua, Patti Campbell, Kathy McCullough, and Pam Wilson

Teachers can deliver functional skills instruction within integrated settings to meet the diverse learning needs of students. By focusing on key elements, educators can design instructional programs that promote the development of functional skills in general education classrooms and community settings. The key elements are: collaborative planning for individual students with disabilities, curricular alignment, teacher/family preparation, creative and flexible teaming, and ongoing implementation support.

Dorothea Fuqua is the principal of Holz Elementary School in Charleston, West Virginia. She has a B.A. in elementary education and special education and an M.A. in educational administration. With 29 years of experience in education, she assisted in the development and administration of one of the first inclusion preschool programs in Kanawha County. She also implemented a full inclusion program at the Holz Elementary School.

Patti Campbell has been a special education teacher for 21 years. She participated in the development and implementation of an inclusive education program at Holz Elementary School. Her master's degree in guidance and counseling is from Marshall University.

Kathy McCullough is the mother of four daughters, the youngest of whom has Angelman Syndrome. She received a B.A. in psychology from Occidental College and a master's in business administration from the University of Southern California. Currently she is the parent representative on the West Virginia Early Intervention Interagency Coordinating Council.

Pam Wilson is a classroom aide at the Holz Elementary School in Charleston, West Virginia. She has several years of experience as an aide and assists in programs dealing with behavior modification and curriculum adaptation, particularly as related to inclusion of students with severe special education needs.

This essay focuses on the key element of collaborative planning. Collaborative teams are essential if students with disabilities are to be included in regular school and community environments. Pooling the expertise, perspectives, and resources of a variety of team members is essential to the design and implementation of functional skills instruction in integrated settings.

Teams must be flexible when planning for individual students. They should keep in mind that an IEP is a working document that reflects a student's current educational program. It must be modified throughout the year as the student's functional needs and abilities change in integrated settings.

Thus educational needs and functional skill priorities must be determined individually for each student. Team members who know the student best must collaborate in making decisions about individual program priorities based on individual, family, school, and community characteristics. This individualization of educational priorities can help to ensure the most appropriate and relevant use of instructional time.

In addition, the targeted skills must be referenced to performance demands in actual environments. Functional skills are useful only if they can be demonstrated in typical daily environments and activities. By conducting an inventory of the demands and opportunities in regular education classes and observing how the student functions in those classes, the IEP team can identify both priority functional skills and the regular class contexts in which they can be demonstrated.

Just as students need time to learn and integrate new concepts into their skill repertoires, so do teachers. General education teachers need to understand the unique learning needs of students with disabilities. They need to understand the curricular and instructional strategies of special education, including how to develop and deliver functional skills instruction; and they need to understand the intricacies and communication patterns of home/school collaboration.

Special education teachers need the opportunity to develop a thorough understanding of the general educator's classes in which students with disabilities may receive functional skill instruction. They need to be aware of the learning needs, styles, and activities of the students in general education class settings; the expectations of the curriculum for that class; the instructional strategies used; and the typical communication patterns used between home and school. This awareness is necessary to determine where and how functional skills can best be taught, as well as to develop the support that will most likely help students with disabilities succeed.

Parents also need to understand the communication patterns of home/school collaboration, and they need to understand their role as a team member in promoting functional skill development. Parents are acutely aware of their children's needs related to functional skill development. They must learn how to share their knowledge with teachers.

Seven Steps to Support Functional Skills Instruction

Teamwork among regular educators, special education teachers, support personnel, parents, and peers is critical to the success of integrated education programs. As IEP teams strive to make goals and objectives relevant and functional, they must have a clear picture of the outcomes desired for individual students — that is, a vision of these students participating in typical school, home, community, and work environments. The planning process discussed here is intended to guide collaborative teams through a process that builds on the individual student's strengths.

Step 1: Identify the Student Support Team

The first step of the planning process is to identify the student support team. Its members are those individuals who have active involvement, interest, responsibility, or expertise in the individual student's program. This includes the family, general education teachers, special education teachers, appropriate related services personnel, and the principal. Other team members may be selected for or advise the support team as needed, depending on the needs of the student and the team. These other members might include a school counselor, school psychologist, classroom aide, student peer, or specialist. The support team provides a vehicle for creative problem solving, regular home-school communication, consistent support to teachers and parents, and program coordination.

The student support team plans and assesses the ongoing instruction for a student who has challenging needs. Initially, the entire support team should meet to plan the student's program. As the program becomes established, it is possible that only the teachers and parents may meet. The team may need to meet weekly, but it may be possible to decrease meeting frequency as the team becomes more efficient in the planning process.

The student support team may be larger than the student's IEP committee, though individuals from the student's IEP committee are members of the student support team. For example, a student's friend, a grandmother, or a consultant may be part of the student's support team but are not required members of the student's IEP committee.

Step 2: Conduct the MAPS Process

The McGill Action Planning System (MAPS) is a useful tool for identifying important functional goals for the student. It helps develop an understanding of who the student really is, instead of knowing the child only by his or her label.

MAPS, developed by Marsha Forest at McGill University, is not intended to be used for every student with disabilities. However, different aspects of MAPS can be developed for different students, depending on the age and needs of the student. The MAPS process should be conducted at crucial transition points in a student's education (for example, preschool to elementary school, middle to high school, and high school to adulthood).

It is important that the MAPS session not be confused with the special education IEP process. MAPS is intended to develop a working process for program development based on a common understanding among those people who know the student best.

Thus the group that conducts the MAPS process should be composed of the student, family, friends, teachers, and other individuals who are significant in the student's life

For a student the MAPS process can include identifying his or her strengths and weaknesses in each academic area. However, it also can focus on the student's whole life, not just his or her participation in school. This can help the team determine important functional goals in order to meet the student's needs in those settings. The functional goals will become part of the student's IEP.

Step 3: Develop, Review, or Revise the IEP Goals and Objectives

The next step of the planning process is to convene an IEP committee meeting to determine the functional skills to be addressed in the inclusive classroom and other school and community environments. The IEP committee may determine that additional assessments must be completed in order to evaluate the student's current abilities, or the committee may determine that the current IEP contains such an extensive list of objectives that it is cumbersome as a planning tool or the objectives are irrelevant. The question for the team to ask is, "What would really make a difference in the quality of this student's life?" or "What are the most important skills for the student to learn now?"

The MAPS process will serve as the foundation for the development of the goals and objectives for the student. Some of the needs identified in MAPS will become goals in the IEP.

Step 4: Complete the Curriculum Matrix

In this step, the student's support team completes a curriculum matrix in order to identify the interface between the student's functional goals and objectives and the opportunities for achieving these in the general education classroom. To ensure that opportunities for instruction are addressed in a variety of settings, the team must identify all settings in which the student will be participating. Particularly as students move into secondary schools, their range of learning environments will expand to include a variety of community locations.

The matrix is completed by listing the skills described in the IEP on one axis and the classroom activities on the other axis. The team then decides which skills can be taught logically and appropriately during which classroom activities by placing an X in the corresponding columns. The completed matrix provides a graphic representation of all of the opportunities for functional skills instruction to take place.

		Worksheet for: _____								
Individual Educational Plan/Curriculum/Environment Matrix										
		Regular Education Class Schedule						Additional Environments		
IEP Goals	Daily Agenda									

The matrix will help identify skill areas that are not addressed in the everyday routine of the classroom. The team then must decide what alternative activities and environments might be appropriate to meet the student's needs. For example, a student may need specific training in using a cane because of visual impairment. While transition periods during the day may provide some time for practice (going to lunch, going to the bus, etc.), no classroom activity really fits with direct instruction of mobility. When such mismatch occurs, the teaching team must decide how, when, where, and by whom the student will receive direct instruction in the skill.

The curriculum matrix is used only when students are not at grade level and their needs differ from the goals of the rest of the class. This is often a very enlightening activity for all team members. As they see how many opportunities there are for students to learn and to practice skills throughout the day (even though they may be at a very different level from other students in the class), team members realize that students with very different abilities can learn from the same activities as other students in the classes. Teachers also begin to realize that mastery of the particular activities is not expected for many students with disabilities; rather, the expectations for what some students will learn may be very different from what others in the classroom will learn.

One area of concern, especially among special education teachers, is how the students will master functional community-referenced skills (for example, riding a city bus, shopping, using a bank, eating in a restaurant, working in community jobs). While general education teachers realize the value of community-referenced learning for typical students, the focus of community-referenced learning in general education programs is on skill application and interest assessment. The challenge is how to integrate the two curricula.

Step 5: Develop the Daily Schedule

In order for teachers to have a clear picture of a typical day in the classroom for the student with diverse needs, it is essential that teachers and parents, if possible, develop a daily schedule. That schedule should identify classroom activities by content areas, goals to be worked on during the class or period, activity suggestions, individual accommodations (environmental, social, curricular), and staff responsibilities and other supports for the student. It is not enough to simply identify opportunities for instruction as represented by the curriculum matrix. The daily schedule should take into account when instruction will occur (frequency, duration, time of day), when practice will occur (to facilitate skill mastery across settings), and who will be responsible for instruction, data collection, and materials accommodation.

The support team may want more detailed information about the structure of the classroom prior to determining the student's daily schedule. An ecological/functional assessment can identify the demands of the class in terms of physical, communicative, and academic requirements. Accommodations then can be made to overcome barriers to participation.

There are educational and instructional differences inherent between planning for an elementary or a secondary student. The generic planning process is the same, but there are some considerations at each level that should be addressed. One of the main issues that will affect planning is schedule flexibility. A typical elementary team may have one general education teacher who is responsible for all the curricular implementation decisions. This is beneficial for planning and monitoring, but it can constrict curricular options. The secondary school offers some flexibility for curricular options (that is, what classes are available), but it has some limitations for planning, development, and so on. At the secondary level, content-specific goals for each class must be clarified. In addition, the various teachers on the team will have limited time to develop an understanding of a student's functional needs, especially because it can be difficult for the entire team to meet on a regular basis at the secondary level. However, each instructor should have an understanding of the student's goals in their specific content area.

Developing the daily schedule provides a basis for the student's educational program. But this step of the planning process should never be thought of as being completed. It is an ongoing process and is expected to change through the year, just as classroom activities change. However, it does provide a framework for organization, communication, and the clarification of responsibilities.

Step 6: Provide Strong, Ongoing Implementation Support

Once the support team has completed a collaborative plan for meeting a student's functional needs in a general education setting, the next step is to implement the program and provide the ongoing supports that will ensure success. It is essential that general education teachers be supported on a daily basis in implementing the program. Just as the student's plan is individualized, so is special education support. The key to successful individualization is to accommodate existing support structures within the school. Examples of strategies that build on naturally occurring supports follow.

Social Peer Support: Nondisabled peers often are some of the best problem-solvers and supporters for achieving the successful integration of students with disabilities. However, building social supports within schools and classrooms must be well planned.

Homerooms can provide peer support for instruction and solving problems. For a student with special needs, this structure provides a good base for support. The team can identify and accommodate individual needs, such as learning how to frame questions, how to organize materials, and how to adjust rules in social games and activities.

Some students with special needs may require additional social supports, such as the Circle of Friends strategy. This provides an extra level of social support for students who may need more intensive assistance with program orientation, friendship development, and problem solving. The circle is facilitated by a member of the student's support team and meets on a regular basis to foster friendships and commitment among all of the students.

In the classroom, such peer-mediated strategies as cooperative learning and peer tutors foster cooperative, heterogeneous groupings of students. Such groups help students understand and value diversity. Again, individualized accommodations for a student with special needs must be developed by the support team.

Instructional Support: The focus on applied learning for all students helps to create many opportunities for functional skill instruction in general education classes. For example, projects, hands-on activities, thematic approaches, and multimedia presentations are common across the curriculum. However, the teaching team must still plan together to design activities that are meaningful for all students and identify the instructional accommodations for certain students. A framework for designing such adaptations include the following options:

- A different format.
- The same content but less of it.
- Streamlining the sequence of content.
- Partial participation by the student with disabilities.
- Instruction targeting the same skills but using different materials.
- Instruction geared toward a different skill level but using the same materials.
- The same activity but targeting different skills.
- Skills embedded in the activity.
- Different response to the same instruction.
- Different amount of personal assistance.
- Different instruction, different materials, different environments.

This support can help create better instruction and meaningful participation for all students. In addition, it guides the team in designing the least intrusive curricular and instructional modifications necessary to work on the student's priority goals and objectives.

Home/School Collaboration and Support: Communication between home and school takes on added importance when promoting functional skill development. Since most functional skills are used in the home or community, parents often are acutely aware of their son's or daughter's needs in this area. Furthermore, family members are often in an ideal position to evaluate and support performance of functional skills in real settings. Thus communication between home and school is critical. Such methods as weekly notes or daily journals that share information about school activities and student performance can provide the foundation for establishing strong, effective communication between home and school.

Step 7: Evaluate Student Progress and Needs

The last step is to assess the individual student's performance of functional skills within the integrated setting. How do we know that successful learning and social experiences are occurring for the student? How do we know that the supports are effective in meeting the student's needs? The support team cannot make decisions regarding adjustments to the student's educational program unless data are collected.

Data collection is driven by the student's functional IEP goals and objectives. The criteria, methods, and schedules for evaluation are determined for each functional IEP objective and documented on the student's IEP. These data are used by the support team to communicate the child's progress to his or her parents and by the IEP committee to determine the levels of performance for the next IEP. Evaluations also serve a monitoring function for determining whether the IEP is being implemented and whether it is appropriate.

When evaluating a student's mastery of functional skills across integrated settings, data collection procedures must be easily managed and unobtrusive. Examples of methods for collecting data are narrative entries in a journal, anecdotal reports, student portfolios, assessment worksheets, self-monitoring data sheets, charts and graphs, home-school communication, and pre/post measurement. Data should be collected routinely, and their generalizability across different environments must be considered.

Resources

Black, J.; Meyer, L.H.; D'Aquanni, M.; and Giugno, M. *Guidelines for Designing Curricular and Instructional Modifications to Address IEP Objectives in General Education.* Syracuse: Syracuse University, New York Partnership for Statewide Systems Change Project, 1994.

Deschenes, C.; Eberling, D.; and Sprague, J. *Adapting Curriculum and Instruction in Inclusive Classrooms: A Teacher's Desk Reference.* Bloomington: Center for School and Community Integration, Institute for the Study of Developmental Disabilities, Indiana University, 1994.

Dover, W. *The Inclusion Facilitator*. Manhattan, Kans.: Master Teacher, 1994.

Ford, A.; Schnorr, R.; Meyer, L.; Davern, L.; Black, J.; and Dempsey, P. *The Syracuse Community-Referenced Curriculum Guide*. Baltimore: Paul H. Brookes, 1989.

Leroy, B.; Osbuck, T.; and England, J. *Facilitator Guides to Inclusive Education*. Detroit: Wayne State University, Inclusive Community Press, 1994.

Neary, T.; Halvorsen, A.; Kronberg, R.; and Kelly, D. *Curriculum Adaptation for Inclusive Classrooms*. San Francisco: California Research Institute, San Francisco State University, 1992.

Parent Educational Advocacy Training Center. *Keys to Inclusion*. Alexandria, Va., 1994.

Peterson, M.; Leroy, B.; Field, S.; and Wood, P. "Community-Referenced Learning in Inclusive Schools: Effective Curriculum for All Students." In *Curriculum Consideration in Inclusive Classrooms*, edited by S. Stainback and W. Stainback. Baltimore: Paul H. Brookes, 1992.

Schnorr, R.; Ford, A.; Davern, L.; Park-Lee, S.; and Meyer, L. *The Syracuse Curriculum Revision Manual: A Group Process for Developing a Community-Referenced Curriculum Guide*. Baltimore: Paul H. Brookes, 1989.

West Virginia Department of Education. *Developing Quality Individualized Education Programs*. Charleston, W.V., 1993.

York, J.; Doyle, M.; and Kronberg, R. "A Curriculum Development Process for Inclusive Classrooms." *Focus on Exceptional Children* 25, no. 4 (1992): 1-16.

York, J., and Vandercook, T. "Designing an Integrated Program for Learners with Severe Disabilities." *Teaching Exceptional Children* 23, no. 2 (1991): 22-28.

Inclusion: Vision, Theory, and Practice

by Dick Sobsey, Bev Ray, and Heather Raymond

Successful inclusion requires the integration of a meaningful vision, a research foundation, and practical strategies. Without a meaningful and unified vision of the purpose for educating all children, education loses its direction and becomes subject to political expediency. Without the support of research, inclusion remains vulnerable to arguments that it is driven only by advocacy and not by excellence. Without practical strategies for implementation, inclusion remains an ideal that cannot be applied to the real world.

A Meaningful Vision

Public education has the same mission for all children: to prepare children for adult roles in our society. Academic excellence is not an end in itself, but one part of preparing students for par-

Dick Sobsey is a professor of educational psychology and director of the JP Das Developmental Disabilities Centre at the University of Alberta in Canada. He trains teachers and other professionals to work with students with severe and multiple disabilities. He is the father of two children, including a son with a severe developmental disability who attends a regular classroom in his fully inclusive neighborhood school.

Bev Ray is a family support advocate with the Alberta Association for Community Living. She also is mother to a school-aged child with a developmental disability who attends a fully inclusive classroom.

Heather Raymond is an assistant principal in Edmonton, Alberta. She has worked as a consultant and regular classroom teacher in a variety of inclusive school environments. She has presented at numerous universities and conferences throughout Canada and other parts of the globe. Raymond is an active volunteer with the Canadian Associations for Community Living, which supports the concept of community living for all individuals.

ticipation in community life. Academic, vocational, social, and citizenship skills all must be elements of every student's school experience, though some schools may focus more on one element than another. These ideas are not new, nor are they radical. They have been fundamental to public education since the early part of the 20th century.

Schools not only must prepare students to participate in the community, the school also must be a living part of that community. Children cannot be prepared for genuine participation in society if their schools exclude them from participation in the most age-appropriate domain of these very communities. Segregated education can prepare children only for an isolated life outside the mainstream of society. Just as it would be absurd to remove students from the water in order to teach them to swim, it is absurd to envision the preparation of students for roles in our society without immersing them in it.

A Research Foundation

Modern special education began in the 1950s. In 1949 Paul R. Fuller first described the application of operant procedures to a human being, describing how an adolescent with severe and multiple disabilities who had previously been considered incapable of any learning could be conditioned to request drinks by raising his hand. Applied behavior analysis, or behaviorism, developed from Fuller's brief case study; and behaviorism became the major influence on contemporary special education.

Applied behavior analysis proved to be an extremely powerful and useful tool, but its misapplication also created new problems. As research was taken out of the laboratory and applied to schools, special education classrooms began to take on the atmosphere of the laboratory. While Skinner, as the primary proponent of behaviorism, was clear about the distinction between the laboratory and real life, many of his followers failed to grasp that distinction. Skinner suggested that the researcher in a laboratory had total (experimental) control. The effect of intervention was studied under artificial conditions. However, Skinner also understood that, in the real world, everyone does and should have control.

When applied to special education classrooms, experimental control often meant teaching one-on-one in cubicles that would keep out distractions. Learning was often successful in the narrow, artificial conditions provided by special education, but it commonly failed to generalize to any situation in which it would actually have value. In addition, gains commonly faded when the intensive programs were faded out. Behaviorists attempted to answer this with additional programming components to teach maintenance and generalization. In fact, many of the new generalization strategies were exact antitheses of the behavioral methods used to teach skills in the first place. By the 1970s many of the experts in applied behavior analysis who had advocated the artificial controls of the special education classroom were calling for special education classrooms to duplicate the attributes of regular classrooms that special education classrooms had been designed to eliminate.

Of course, there were many other factors that led to the growth in special educational placements. For example, the 1957 launching of Sputnik led to the National Defense Education Act of 1958, which made education a priority for national security. While the primary goal of the National Defense Education Act was to assist the highest-achieving students, funds also went to special education. This was done partly because of a legitimate concern that all students should benefit; but there also was an implicit understanding that children with learning difficulties would get more help and, at the same time, be gotten out of the way of more competent students. Most of the money for students with special needs was used to create segregated classrooms.

While a variety of forces fueled the development of special education placements, research failed to show the value of such placements. While many studies showed that this or that special education program produced some specific gain in a very specific area, research rarely showed advantages to special education placements. In fact, it often documented that special education produced poorer results for students with special needs than did simply leaving the students in the regular classroom.

For example, Goldstein, Moss, and Jordan (1965) found that in the "ideal" special education class, students learned no more arithmetic and less reading than they learned when placed in a regular classroom. In a classic review of research, Dunn analyzed the existing literature and found that students with mild mental handicaps "made as much or more progress in regular grades as they do in special classes" (1968, p. 8).

The failure to show the superiority of segregated special education has been very consistent. For example, a major review of the research on ability grouping found that homogeneous groups did not produce results superior to those of heterogeneous groups (Dar and Resh 1986). Three major meta-analyses have compared special education placements to regular education placements for students with special needs. In each study special education placements were associated with inferior social adjustment and inferior learning (Baker 1994; Carlberg and Kavale 1980; Wang, Anderson, and Bram 1985).

According to the *Handbook of Special Education:*

> Little evidence exists supporting the efficacy of special education or the development of differential programs as a result of the assessment-placement process. Presently, programs for students with mildly handicapping conditions are typically implemented independently of assessment information, irrespectively of less restrictive educational options, and entirely without regard to empirical outcomes. (Epps and Tindal 1987, p. 243)

The empirical evidence favors inclusive education. Why, then, should we consider segregated alternatives? Is it because the cost of inclusion is too high? Is it because the education of students without disabilities suffers as a result of the presence of students with special needs?

Again, empirical studies have attempted to answer these questions. A review of studies on the effects of inclusion on children without disabilities in inclusive classrooms (Staub and Peck 1995) demonstrates three things. First, there have been too few studies to draw clear and final conclusions. Second, the research that has been done has shown no negative effects on learning or social behavior of children without disabilities. Third, positive effects on social behavior (for example, more cooperative behavior) and attitudes (for example, greater acceptance of diversity) have been demonstrated.

The results of cost-benefit studies have been somewhat mixed, but most show that the instructional costs for inclusive education are not more, and may be significantly less, than those for special placements (Roahrig 1995). In addition, there are clear indications that inclusive education has lower noninstructional costs, particularly for transportation, than does segregated education. One controlled study comparing the costs of inclusive education with special education classes matched students on needs and other assessment variables. Results indicated that inclusive education was 13% less expensive and that students learned just as much as did special education students (Halvorsen, Neary, Hunt, and Piuma 1995). Even in those exceptional studies that identify special costs associated with inclusion, the authors generally suggest that those may be startup costs but that inclusion is cost-effective in the longer term (McLaughlin and Warren 1994).

Can we conclude that inclusion is always the best and least expensive alternative? Perhaps we can, but a few cautions are required. First, more research is needed to clarify the relationship between intensive educational intervention and placement. While research to date demonstrates that segregated placements generally have hurt more than they have helped, it has not clearly shown that individualized and intensive learning programs lack merit. We believe that students who have special needs can and often do benefit from individualized programs and that inclusion should not be interpreted as an alternative to these programs but as a directive to ensure that these programs are provided in mainstream environments.

Second, while research clearly demonstrates that the vast majority of students currently served in segregated environments probably would do better in inclusive settings, this cannot be interpreted to apply to each and every individual. The nature of group-comparison research allows us to conclude that if all students with special needs were served in regular classrooms, they would learn more and be better socially adjusted than if all were served in segregated classrooms. It does not guarantee that there are no individuals or even small subgroups for whom the opposite is true.

Third, cost comparisons must be made on the basis of systems, not individuals. Inclusive education typically costs less when an entire district or system is inclusive. The costs for some individual students will increase, and the costs for others will decrease. Unfortunately, many systems have moved toward inclusion for the individuals who create cost savings but resist inclusion for those who do not.

Fourth, the move toward inclusion must be done through the redeployment of resources, not the elimination of programs. Unfortunately, there have been frequent indications of downsizing under the banner of inclusion. Students formerly placed in special education classrooms are placed in already overcrowded classrooms without needed resources and support. The result is often poor education and teacher resistance to inclusion. While we believe that teachers should support inclusion and welcome students with special needs, we also believe that they have a right and a responsibility to demand that the resources and supports are available to make inclusive education successful.

Practical Strategies

There are a number of good resources for planning inclusive education programs. The McGill Action Planning System (MAPS) is one that has proven very useful (Forest and Lusthaus 1989). It was developed as a tool to help schools include students with disabilities in the regular classroom. MAPS treats the school as a community and emphasizes that communities are built on positive collaborative relationships. MAPS is particularly useful in developing long-term goals that become the basis for the Individualized Educational Program (IEP). MAPS begins with a series of questions that help clarify what parents and others involved (including the student) see as hopes, fears, and possibilities for the future and uses the answers to identify goals that later will become specific objectives and activities.

An activities matrix is another vital tool for inclusion. The activities matrix includes a schedule of classroom activities in which the entire class will participate and identifies appropriate objectives, instructional strategies, and supports for the student with special needs who participates in these activities. Most students will participate in some activities and work on some of the same objectives without special supports. For other activities and objectives, some supports may be required. For yet others, students may work on entirely different objectives within the context of the same activities.

Instructional delivery also is likely to change as teachers move toward the greater diversity of inclusive education. Two instructional approaches commonly associated with inclusive teaching are multi-level instruction and cooperative learning. Multi-level instruction is closely associated with the activities matrix. It individualizes the curriculum objectives and instructional approaches within specific curriculum areas. This is an approach used intuitively by many teachers, who save harder tasks for more advanced students while offering easier tasks to those who require them. Multi-level instruction provides the means for extending and refining this approach.

Cooperative learning uses teams or pairs of students working together on a particular task or activity. Rather than forcing students to compete, it rewards team members for finding ways to work together (O'Connor and Jenkins 1996).

Teachers also need consultation and support. Specialist personnel who formerly taught in segregated settings may now act as consultants to assist teachers. Considering the wide range of knowledge that may be required by teachers, the availability of appropriate consultants may be critical to good practice. Classroom assistants also are important for some successful inclusion of students. Nevertheless, when used to excess or used improperly, classroom assistants may actually hinder inclusion. Classroom assistants generally are used to greatest advantage when they are seen as a resource for the entire classroom, rather than as responsible for only the child with special needs. Their primary role should be to facilitate the involvement of students with special needs into the classroom's activities, rather than to occupy the student with alternative activities.

These are only a few of the practical strategies that can be used for successful inclusion. Many more exist, and new ones are identified frequently. There is much more to be learned about what makes good inclusive education, but there is already more than an adequate base from which to proceed.

References

Baker, E.T. "Meta-Analytic Evidence for Non-Inclusive Educational Practices: Does Educational Research Support Current Practices for Special Needs Students?" Doctoral dissertation. Temple University, 1994.

Carlberg, C., and Kavale, K. "The Efficacy of Special Versus Regular Class Placement for Exceptional Children: A Meta-Analysis." *Journal of Special Education* 14 (1980): 295-309.

Dar, Y., and Resh, N. *Classroom Composition and Pupil Achievement.* New York: Gordon and Breach, 1986.

Dunn, L.M. "Special Education for the Mildly Retarded — Is Much of It Justifiable?" *Exceptional Children* 35 (1968): 5-22.

Epps, S., and Tindal, G. "The Effectiveness of Differential Programming in Serving Students with Mild Handicaps: Placement Options and Instructional Programming." In *Handbook of Special Education: Research and Practice*, Vol. 1, edited by M.C. Wang, M.C. Reynolds, and H.J. Walberg. Oxford: Pergamon Press, 1987.

Forest, M., and Lusthaus, E. "Promoting Educational Equality for All Students: Circles and MAPS." In *Educating All Students in the Mainstream of Regular Education*, edited by W. Stainback, S. Stainback, and M. Forest. Baltimore: Paul H. Brookes, 1989.

Goldstein, H.; Moss, J.; and Jordan, J. *The Efficacy of Special Class Training on the Development of Mentally Retarded Children.* U.S. Office of Education Project No. 619. Champaign-Urbana: University of Illinois, 1965.

Halvorsen, A.T.; Neary, T.; Hunt, P.; and Piuma, C. "A Cost-Benefit Comparison of Inclusive and Integrated Classes in One California District." In *California Peers Outreach Project: Application and Replication of Inclusive Models at the Local Level, Final Report*, by L. Sandoval et al. Sacramento: California State Department of Education, Division of Special Education, 1995. ERIC Document Reproduction Service Number ED 393 249.

McLaughlin, M.J., and Warren, S.H. "The Costs of Inclusion." *School Administrator* 51, no. 10 (1994): 8-12, 16-19.

O'Connor, R., and Jenkins, J.R. "Cooperative Learning as an Inclusion Strategy: A Closer Look." *Exceptionality* 6, no. 1 (1996): 29-51.

Roahrig, P.L. "Fiscal Analysis of a Special Education Inclusion Program." *ERS Spectrum* 13, no. 1 (1995): 18-24.

Staub, D., and Peck, C. "What Are the Outcomes for Nondisabled Students?" *Educational Leadership* 52, no. 4 (1995): 36-40.

Wang, M.C.; Anderson, K.A.; and Bram, P.J. *Toward an Empirical Data Base on Mainstreaming: A Research Synthesis of Program Implementation and Effects.* Pittsburgh: Learning Research and Development Center, University of Pittsburgh, 1985.

Inclusive Education:
A Consciousness of Caring

by George Flynn

We are beginning to discover that education at its best — these profound human transactions called knowing, teaching, and learning — are not about just information and are not about just getting jobs They are about healing and transformation. They are about wholeness. They are about empowerment, liberation, and transcendence. They are about "reclaiming the vitality of life," as Parker Palmer said in a recent presentation:

> Why is it that, in our time, words like education, teaching, learning have so little life-giving power? Why are these words and the things they point to so flat, so dull, so banal? (1997*a*)

We know that there are several answers to these questions, including:

- The 19th-century industrial model of schooling that is still with us;
- The diminishing effects of professionalism in teacher training; and
- The way education has devolved into political rhetoric and, to a large extent, serves the purposes of power.

George Flynn is a senior staff associate with the Center for Social Development and Education at the University of Massachusetts, Boston, where he is involved in research and training. He is also executive director of the SEEM Collaborative, a nonprofit support system for eight school districts on the North Shore. Previously he was the director of special education for the largest school system in Canada and executive director of the Association for Persons with Severe Handicaps (TASH).

But how do we reclaim this from the essentially depressive mode of knowing that honors only data, logic, analysis, and a systematic disconnection of self from the world, self from others. This is the basis for exclusion; and until we deal with this, we cannot have inclusion.

We no longer can afford an education system that refuses to get engaged with the "mess," the mass of real people living real lives. We must be willing to join life where people live it. The students do not care how much we know until they know how much we care, and we show that we care when we join them in life where they live it.

This is the context within which inclusive education is to be considered. Inclusion into what? For what purpose?

One of the great failures of education is reductionism, the destruction of that previous "otherness" by cramming everything into categories that we find comfortable, ignoring data, ignoring voices, ignoring information, ignoring even simple facts that do not fit into our boxes, because we do not have, or have not developed, a respect for otherness. In fact, we have a fear of otherness. In our culture, if the difference between me and the other is too great, I have learned to get rid of the other by using a category, a dismissal, or a word of some sort that renders the other irrelevant to my life.

Inclusive education has to be realized. It cannot be standardized; it cannot be dictated; it cannot be forced. Inclusion has to be realized through a change of heart, through a raising of consciousness.

We will have to re-invent our schools. We will have to come to new understanding, and we will have to exchange some popular prevailing beliefs for new beliefs. We will move away from competition toward cooperation until we have achieved the proper balance. We will move away from individualism toward community until we have achieved the proper balance. We will move from an ethos of self-performance to an ethos of empowering the group. We will move from our current heavy reliance on experts to a greater reliance on the collective wisdom of a creative and humble community. In each case, our objective is to arrive at the correct balance and not to destroy one for the other. It is not either/or; it is both — in the correct balance.

We will move to another level of consciousness because it is with consciousness that we, and the children, are moved to engage in dialogue with others, to reach toward what is not, what might be, what seems decent, valuable, humane. The consciousness of alienation and meaninglessness that is related to loneliness, despair, and seeking solace in drugs, hedonism, violence, and materialism, and which prevails in our culture today, will be replaced by another consciousness. The new level of consciousness will be a consciousness of caring, compassion, and justice that is related to notions of beauty and sacredness of life itself and the centrality of the idea of dignity for all. We will come to understand that our challenge is not to deepen our separation from each other but to strengthen our connections while safeguarding and celebrating our differences.

Inclusive education is not a program; it is not a placement. It is a way of being in the world that is life-giving, that lifts people up, that seeks to construct a unity out of difference, that always demonstrates a "simple respect" for otherness. As the Quakers say:

> be present to each other in the right spirit, speaking our truth gently and simply, listening respectfully and attentively to the truth of others, grounded in our own experience and expanded by experiences that are not yet ours, compassionate toward that which we do not yet understand, not only as a kindness to others but for the sake of our growth and our students and the transformation of education. (Palmer 1997b)

It is in this spirit that we come to understand that inclusive education is not a special education issue. It is a general education issue. It is about creative classrooms across the nation that are places of hope, where students and teachers, through their rich interactions, gain glimpses of the kind of society we could live in and where students learn the academic and critical skills needed to make it a reality. The questions become:

- Have you ever had such glimpses?
- What are the academic and critical skills needed?

Inclusive classrooms are grounded in the lives of our students. An inclusive classroom is one where, first and foremost, there is a simple but profound respect for all students. There will be respect for their innate curiosity and their capacity to learn regardless of the level at which that occurs. Every aspect of the curriculum will be rooted in the needs and experiences of the students. The class will be about the students' lives, as well as the subject, regardless of the subject matter being dealt with.

The students — all of the students — will have facilitated and nonfacilitated experiences that probe and enlighten how their lives are connected to the broader society or limited by that society. They will have experiences, some intended and some not, where they will discover how they are connected to each other or limited by the other and what appropriate responses might be to such situations.

Inclusive classrooms focus on the development of critical skills. In inclusive classrooms questions are asked, such as:

- Whose voices are heard when we make decisions?
- Who benefits and who suffers from those decisions?

Students learn to pose and to respond to essential, critical questions. They learn to "talk back" to the world. Their learning is linked to real-world issues, which, again, grounds them in their own lives. Real issues, such as critiquing advertising, cartoons, literature, legislative decisions, job structures, movies, agricultural practices, and other critical issues of the day become the base for the whole curriculum.

Inclusive classrooms also are multicultural classrooms. The current curriculum in most classrooms has been developed from the perspective of the dominant culture. The standpoint of the dominant group prevails, often leading to an inherent disregard for the lives of women, the lives of working people, the lives of people of color, and the lives of people with disabilities.

In contrast, the curriculum in an inclusive classroom would rigorously engage the students in multicultural issues, in anti-racist issues, and in pro-justice issues. The students would critique the roots of inequality at all levels: the classroom, the district structure, structures in the larger society. They would come to understand that inclusive education is not a disability issue; rather, it is about dealing effectively with injustice in any area of life.

Inclusive classrooms are participatory and experiential. In inclusive classrooms students are provoked to engage in democratic experiences where their democratic capacities are developed. They learn to question effectively, to challenge appropriately, to engage in making real decisions, and to collectively solve problems.

Democratic capacities cannot just be read about or heard about. These concepts have to be experienced first hand through projects, role plays, simulations, mock trials, and so forth. The students come to new understandings and beliefs in powerful ways, through experience and through participation.

Inclusive classrooms are hopeful, joyful, kind, and visionary. Education should be a life-giving force; but too often it is the opposite, death-dealing. Inclusive classrooms are about reclaiming the hope and joy and vision that should exist in effective classrooms by breaking through the essentially depressive current mode of knowing that honors only data, logic, analysis, and a systematic disconnection of self from the world, and self from others.

Inclusive classrooms seek to make all children feel significant and cared about. If students do not feel emotionally and physically safe, they will not share real thoughts and feelings and their conversation will be tiny and often dishonest. Inclusive classrooms engage students in activities that lead them to learn about and to choose to practice trusting and caring for each other. Classrooms, schools, and districts must model the kind of just and democratic society we are envisioning. Teachers and students develop a shared consciousness, a community of conscience

Inclusive classrooms are activist by nature. A critical curriculum in an inclusive classroom should reflect the diversity of people from all cultures who acted to make a difference in the world.

Students draw inspiration from historical and contemporary efforts of people who struggled for justice. We want our students to come to see themselves as truth-tellers and change-makers; and by learning about these qualities in other people who made a difference, historical or contemporary and from all cultures, they are inspired to do so.

We want to develop in our students the desire to critique and then the courage to act. Critique without action can lead to cynicism. The empowerment, the liberation, the transcendence that we hope for from the educational experiences of our students will come to them when they see themselves as truth-tellers and change-makers.

These developments must be encouraged in a critically sensitive way. Critical teaching requires that we admit that we do not know it all. It also requires us to call on culturally diverse colleagues and other community resources for insights. Knowing, teaching, learning is a communal exercise.

Inclusive classrooms are academically rigorous. The successful inclusive classroom not only equips students to change the world but also to successfully maneuver in the one that exists. For example, we work with students to help them "pass the test" at the same time that we help them analyze, critique, and understand the harmful impact of a test-driven curriculum. A critical and activist curriculum speaks directly to valuing vital academic skills that students need.

It is essential that academic rigor be recognized as an essential component of successful inclusive classrooms in order to counteract the often-held perception that the curriculum is "dumbed-down" to accommodate the diversity of learners.

The most important task we have in education today is to formulate and to offer a broad and inclusive discussive framework through which a diversity of people can see the hopes and concerns that they have for themselves and their children. We have to find a way to bring together dissimilar people with distinct, often divergent, interests and concerns so they can find common ground. We must discover ways to nurture the common and discover ways that allow new perspectives and new visions to enrich the present reality. Inclusive classrooms, built on a consciousness of caring, provide the opportunity for this to happen. An inclusive classroom can be a "unity of beings."

References

Palmer, P. "The Grace of Great Things: Reclaiming the Sacred in Knowing, Teaching, and Learning." Presentation at the Spirituality in Education Conference, Naropa Institute, Boulder, Colorado, 30 May - 3 June 1997. a

Palmer, P. "The Grace of Great Things." *Holistic Education Review* 10, no. 3 (1997): 8-16. b

Inclusion: Better Education for All Students

by Thomas P. Lombardi

There is no universally accepted definition for inclusion. And because there is none, it adds to the controversy about inclusion. For the most part, agreement does exist that inclusion involves educating each student with a disability in the school and, when appropriate, the class that the student would have attended if he or she did not have a disability.

A guiding principle behind inclusion is to bring the services to the student, rather than bringing the student to the services. Another, and perhaps of greater significance, is that the student with a disability is fully accepted as part of the student body of that school, with all the rights, privileges, and responsibilities of every other student.

In the United States the federal laws that clearly support inclusionary practices are Section 504 of the Rehabilitation Act, the Individuals with Disabilities Education Act, and the American Disability Act. In Canada, it is clear that there are differences among provinces (as there are among states). However, the major emphasis of Canada's national education is "child-centered learning" (Manzer 1985). Schools are seen to contribute to individual

Thomas P. Lombardi is a professor of special education at West Virginia University. He is the author of numerous articles, chapters, and books, including Phi Delta Kappa fastbacks on inclusion, learning strategies, and issues and trends in special education. Lombardi was named an outstanding teacher by the WVU College of Human Resources and Education three times. He has received recognition by Phi Delta Kappa in the areas of research, service, and leadership and recently received a Fulbright Senior Award to assist in the development of a new special education program at Lusofona University in Lisbon, Portugal.

development by providing learning experiences that meet the complex needs of each individual child. There is a de-emphasis on the ranking and competition that often accompanies different curriculum selection.

Some supporters of full inclusion advocate placing all children with disabilities in general classes regardless of the severity of their problems. Their premise is that all students can be accommodated and to do otherwise is a form of discrimination. Others take a more moderate position regarding inclusion. They feel that for some students with disabilities the general class is not always the best placement. They remind us that, by law, other options must be made available. Still others view inclusion as a step backward to a time when students with disabilities were unable to compete and usually isolated in general classes.

My personal position is to add the adjective "responsible" to "inclusion." Those practicing inclusion must recognize the responsibilities that come with it. Community leaders, school administrators, teachers, parents, and the students themselves all have responsibilities for inclusion. Community leaders must provide the legal, moral, and monetary support associated with responsible inclusion. School administrators must establish a climate in their schools that respects individual differences and allows everyone to help each other. Teachers must learn how to individualize and become creative in their instruction. Parents must become even stronger partners with the schools in supporting inclusion efforts. And students, both the disabled and non-disabled, must commit themselves to forming a wider circle of friends and taking risks to maximize their own learning potential.

Regardless of one's position, more and more students with disabilities are being included in general education classes. According to statistics reported to the U.S. Department of Education the number of students with disabilities in inclusive settings has increased dramatically. In the 1987-88 school year 29% of all students with disabilities received education services in general classes; by 1993-94 the figure was well over 40% (U.S. Department of Education 1996). There is every reason to believe the numbers will continue to increase. In June 1997 President Clinton signed into law the Amendments to the Individuals with Disabilities Education Act (IDEA), designed to strengthen academic expectations and accountability for our nation's 5.4 million students receiving special education services and to reduce barriers that keep them from receiving most, if not all, of their education in general classes.

However, managing the changes necessary for responsible inclusion to work is quite complex. It involves having a vision, skills, incentives, resources, and a plan of action. Without a vision, there is confusion. Without the skills, there is anxiety. Without incentives, the change process will be undermined. Without resources, there will be frustration. And without a plan of action, there will be many false starts.

The Working Forum on Inclusive Schools, a consortium of 10 national education associations, has been studying the issues and potential solutions related to inclusive schools and inclusive schooling. The consortium consists of the American Association of School Administrators, the American Federation of Teachers, the Council for Exceptional Children, the Council of the Great City Schools, the National Association of Elementary School Principals, the National Association of Secondary School Principals, the National Association of State Boards of Education, the National Association of State Directors of Special Education, the National Education Association, and the National School Boards Association. They agreed that characteristics of an inclusive school include flexible learning environments, a sense of community, collaboration and cooperation, new forms of accountability, parents embraced as equal partners, and continued professional development (Working Forum on Inclusive Schools 1994).

Some of the characteristics associated with effective inclusive classrooms include multilevel instruction, teaming, and peer supports (Hammeken 1995). Multilevel instruction allows for different kinds of learning in the same curriculum. Focus is on key concepts to be taught and different ways students can express their understanding of those concepts. Teaming allows the general and special educator to work together. This can include one teacher teaching while the other observes or assists. It might involve parallel teaching, where each teacher instructs half the group using the same or adapted materials. Or it might involve team teaching, where both teachers share the presentation of the lesson to the entire group. Peer support involves students assisting one another as tutors, coaches, or collaborators. Characteristics of inclusive lessons include using advanced organizers, preteaching special vocabulary and major concepts, modeling expected performance, allowing extra time for work completion, using post organizers to summarize, and providing immediate, positive, and corrective feedback (Lombardi 1994).

Educating students with disabilities with their nondisabled peers was one of the major principles of the Education for Handicapped Children Act (Public Law 94-142), now renamed the Individuals with Disabilities Education Act (Public Law 101-476). In letters responding to questions about including children with disabilities into general classes, the U.S. Department of Education has noted that "the regular class in neighborhood schools should be the first-place option for students with disabilities" (Riley 1994). It also should be noted that, legally, placement decisions are made only after a multidisciplinary team meets, determines eligibility and needs, and develops a student's individual education program (IEP). Clearly parents and, when feasible, the student should be involved with placement decisions. One of the foundation court cases, *Sacramento City Unified School District* v. *Holland* (1994), established factors to be considered when educating students with disabilities in general classes. These factors were: Can the student benefit from such placement academically? Can the student benefit socially? and What are placement effects on the teacher and other students?

Recently there has been growing debate about the cost of special education (Irmsher 1996). In the Boston Public Schools, for example, average class size could be reduced from 26 to 13 students if categorical dollars earmarked for special education could be directed to the regular class environment (Odden et al. 1995). The smaller class size would allow a greater degree of individualized teaching for all students.

There is little doubt that implementing responsible inclusion is and will continue to be hard work. The obvious questions are what are the benefits and can they really be achieved?

Some of the benefits to teachers include feeling successful in meeting new challenges, adopting and adapting fresh approaches, and individualizing instruction for all students. Some of the benefits to parents include keeping their child in the neighborhood school, feeling more a part of the community, and developing a greater array of options for their child's future for living and working and enjoying full citizenship. Perhaps of greatest importance are the benefits to our students. Students with disabilities will have the opportunity to form a wider circle of friends, face greater social and academic challenges, and experience satisfaction from full school citizenship. Students without disabilities should be able to appreciate the similarities and differences among people, increase their comfort level around people with disabilities, and learn what it is like to become a helping, caring member of a community.

As for achieving those benefits, there is growing evidence that students with disabilities who have had their education in integrated settings do much better socially, academically, and vocationally than do students with disabilities educated in segregated settings (Piuma 1989; Halversen and Sailor 1990; Corbin 1991; Hunt et al. 1994). And research also indicates that achievement test performance among general education students who were classmates of students with significant disabilities were equivalent or better than a comparison group (Salisbury 1993); and students developed more positive attitudes toward peers with disabilities (California Research Institute 1992; Lombardi et al. 1994).

Despite the growing support for responsible inclusion, there are still many misconceptions, sometimes generated by confusing data collection and reporting. One major example is in the "27th Annual Phi Delta Kappa/Gallup Poll on the Public's Attitudes Toward Public Schools" (Elam and Rose 1995). In that poll, one series of questions dealt with the issue of inclusion of special education students in regular classrooms. The conclusion cited in the report was that the public's clear preference is to place students with learning problems in special classrooms. But that conclusion is very misleading. A review of the four questions asked indicated that the pollsters considered students with physical handicaps, mental handicaps, and learning problems as if they all had the same type of special needs. In addition, there was no acknowledgment of level of disability or the range of options available on a continuum of service placements. Respondents had to choose either a regular class preference or special class preference. Clearly there are a series of placement options between these extremes, including part-time regular placement, resource rooms for short periods of time, and itinerant services. In addition, not all students with disabilities require, are eligible for, or need special education services. A response from the senior author of the poll assured me personally that the next time Phi Delta Kappa addresses the area of special education in such a poll, the authors will engage in greater consultation with special education authorities before drafting their questions. They also invited me to review and comment on the questions before releasing the next poll.

Responsible inclusion for many students with disabilities may involve little more than minor modifications in terms of time, difficulty level, and response to instruction. A smaller number may need to have more significant modifications in terms of how instruction is delivered, levels of support, and even alternative goals. And responsible inclusion involves the recognition that some students with disabilities may need to have some instruction outside of the regular class. One school system in Texas has developed a Count Down to Inclusion Continuum with 41 potentially different program placement considerations for increasing mainstreaming services.

Tests, such as the "Analysis of Classroom and Instructional Demands" (West 1993), are beginning to provide tools to aid in responsible inclusion decisions. The ACID Test identifies and describes teacher expectations, demands, and standards and those student behaviors that are critical for adequate performance in specific classrooms. Once these are determined, better decisions can be made about the potential success of an inclusive placement, as well about the types of interventions and supports that will be necessary for success.

The inclusion movement is not confined to the United States and Canada. A report from the World Conference on Special Needs Education, held in Spain in 1994, affirmed the principle of education for all and specifically endorsed the concept of inclusion for students with special needs (Lombardi and Ludlow 1996). Representatives from 92 countries and 25 international organizations encouraged collaborative efforts among regular and special education personnel in meeting the needs of students at risk for failure, as well as students identified as having disabilities.

There still are many unresolved issues concerning responsible inclusion, such as planning time, teacher/student ratios, new relationships, and needed skills. Responsible inclusion is a program, not a placement. It is not a quick fix but steady work. It requires preservice training, as well as inservice training for all our educators and administrators. And it is not an isolated initiative but a comprehensive reform.

Special education always has been driven by the needs of the individual. As such, it is a model that can serve as the solution to many of our school problems. All students need to have a special education. Their future demands it.

References

California Research Institute. *The Integration of Students with Severe Disabilities: Final Report, Years 1987-1992.* San Francisco: San Francisco State University, 1992.

Corbin, N. "The Impact of Learning Together." *What's Working.* St. Paul: Minnesota Department of Education, 1991.

Elam, S.M., and Rose, L.C. "The 27th Annual Phi Delta Kappa/Gallup Poll of the Public's Attitudes Toward the Public Schools." *Phi Delta Kappan* 77 (September 1995): 41-56.

Halvorsen, A.T., and Sailor, W. "Integration of Students with Severe and Profound Disabilities: A Review of the Research." In *Issues and Research in Special Education: Vol. I*, edited by R. Gaylord-Ross. New York: Teachers College Press, 1990.

Hammeken, P.A. *Inclusion: 450 Strategies for Success.* Minnetonka, Minn.: Peytral, 1995.

Hunt, P.; Farron-Davis, F.; Beckstead, S.; Curtis, B.; and Goetz, L. "Evaluating the Effects of Placement of Students with Severe Disabilities in General Education Versus Special Classes." *Journal of the Association of Persons with Severe Handicaps* 19, no. 3 (1994): 200-14.

Irmsher, K. "Inclusive Education in Practice." *ERIC Review* 4, no. 3 (1996): 18-19.

Lombardi, T.P. *Responsible Inclusion of Students with Disabilities.* Fastback 373. Bloomington, Ind.: Phi Delta Kappa Educational Foundation, 1994.

Lombardi, T.P., and Ludlow, B.L. *Trends Shaping the Future of Special Education.* Fastback 409. Bloomington, Ind.: Phi Delta Kappa Educational Foundation, 1996.

Lombardi, T.P.; Nuzzo, D.L.; Kennedy, K.D.; and Foshay, J. "Perceptions of Parents, Teachers, and Students Regarding an Integrated Education Inclusion Program." *High School Journal* 77 (April/May 1994): 315-21.

Manzer, R.A. *Public Policies and Political Development in Canada.* Toronto: University of Toronto Press, 1985.

Odden, A.; Monk, D.; Yasser, N.; and Picus, L. "The Story of the Education Dollar." *Phi Delta Kappan* 77 (November 1995): 161-68.

Piuma, M.F. *Benefits and Costs of Integrating Students with Severe Disabilities into Regular School Programs: A Study of Money Well Spent.* San Francisco: San Francisco State University Department of Education, 1989.

Riley, Richard. "State of American Education." Speech presented at Georgetown University, 15 February 1994.

Salisbury, D. "Designing and Implementing New Models of Schooling." *International Journal of Educational Research* 19, no. 2 (1993): 99-195.

U.S. Department of Education. *Eighteenth Annual Report to Congress on the Implementation of the Individuals with Disabilities Education Act.* Washington, D.C.: U.S. Government Printing Office, 1996.

West, J.F. "Analysis of Classroom and Instructional Demands." In *Effective Instruction of Difficult-to-Teach Students*, edited by L. Idol and J.F. West. Austin: Pro-Ed, 1993.

Working Forum on Inclusive Schools. *Creating Schools for All Our Students: What 12 Schools Have to Say*. Reston, Va.: Council for Exceptional Children, 1994.